Presented to

....

From

....

Date

....

Forever in Love

I am my beloved's, and my beloved is mine....
SONG OF SOLOMON 6:3

Copyright © 1995
By Word Publishing, Inc.
Dallas, TX 75039

Scripture portions are from *The Holy Bible,
King James Version.*

J. Countryman is a registered trademark of
Word Publishing, Inc.

A J. Countryman Book.

*Design by Koechel Peterson & Associates, Inc.,
Minneapolis, Minnesota*

Library of Congress Cataloging-in-Publication Data

Forever in love.

p. cm.

ISBN 0-8499-5217-4

1. Married people—Prayer-books and devotions—
English.   2. Love—Religious aspects—Christianity—
Prayer-books and devotions—English.

I. Word Publishing
BV4596.M3F67 1995
242'.644–dc20
95-18138 CIP

ISBN: 0-8499-5217-4

Printed and bound in Belgium.

Contents

Learning to Love

All of the gold and silver in the world is not worth as much as the abiding love of another. Give your love as a precious gift to a mate worthy of your care and affection.

GOLD

Yet shall ye be as the wings of a dove covered with silver, and her feathers with yellow gold.

PSALM 68:13

Learning to Love

Let your mate know he
can trust in your loyalty and
fidelity. Trust is one key to
a happy bonding of your love.
Cultivate trust and you
cultivate a fulfilling and
refreshing love life.

TRUST

*The heart of her husband doth
safely trust in her, so that he
shall have no need of spoil.*

PROVERBS 31:11

Learning to Love

Paying homage will bring the shine of love to your mate's eyes. Don't be hesitant to tell of the beauty that is brought to your life by your beloved. Take every opportunity to compliment your loved one.

HOMAGE

Behold, thou art fair, my love; behold, thou art fair; thou hast doves' eyes.

SONG OF SOLOMON 1:15

Learning to Love

Don't withhold the sweetness
of love from your spouse.
Accept the delights of love
with an open hand. Enjoy and
rejoice in the pleasures God
has ordained in marriage.

HONEYCOMB

*My son, eat thou honey, because
it is good; and the honeycomb,
which is sweet to thy taste.*

PROVERBS 24:13

Learning to Love

Virtue is the foundation of
a solid marriage. Let your mate
know he can safely trust his
affection and love to you.
Don't give in to the
temptation to squander
your love in adultery.

VIRTUE

*Who can find a virtuous woman? For
her price is far above rubies.*

PROVERBS 31:10

Learning to Love

An affair begins with the eyes.
Be careful not to let your eyes
deceive you. The one you
desire might look attractive,
but adultery ends in ugly
arguments and hidden guilt.
What looks pleasant in most
cases turns sour and destroys.

WANDERINGS

*Better is the sight of the eyes than the
wandering of the desire: this is also
vanity and vexation of spirit.*

ECCLESIASTES 6:9

Learning to Love

Love is like a garden. The seed
of love is planted, but unless
someone tends the garden
a strong plant will never grow.
Love requires long, hard work.
Today is a good day to start
paying attention to
your beloved.

GARDEN

*Let my beloved come into his garden,
and eat his pleasant fruits.*

SONG OF SOLOMON 4:16

Learning to Love

Words can build a relationship
or destroy it. Let your words
be those that build honesty
and love between you and
your beloved. Speak from
your heart and your love will
be healthier for it.

WORDS

Pleasant words are as a honeycomb,
sweet to the soul, and health
to the bones.

PROVERBS 16:24

Learning to Love

May your nights be filled with
the comfort of a binding love.
Don't let the troubles of your
day intrude upon the coziness
of a night spent in the
arms of your beloved.

NIGHTTIME

*Come, let us take our fill of love
until the morning: let us solace
ourselves with loves.*

PROVERBS 7:18

Learning to Love

Love needs a seal set upon it.
A seal says this love of yours is
important to you. It says you
will be true and faithful to
your beloved. Love your mate
with confidence.

SEAL

*Set me as a seal upon thine heart, as
a seal upon thine arm; for love is
strong as death. . . .*

SONG OF SOLOMON 8:6

Learning to Love

Kindness builds love. Act toward your beloved in a kindly manner that seeks the good of the one you love. Show your love by thinking of your mate first—before yourself. You will find a reward beyond your wildest imagination if your love follows this noble path.

KINDLY

And his soul clave unto Dinah the daughter of Jacob, and he loved the damsel, and spake kindly unto the damsel.

GENESIS 34:3

17

Learning to Love

True love weathers every storm and outlasts every trouble. Make your love the kind of love that shelters you forever. Build a relationship with your beloved that will comfort you in your old age.

FOREVER

Let her be as the loving hind and pleasant roe; let her breasts satisfy thee at all times; and be thou ravished always with her love.

PROVERBS 5:19

Learning to Love

Arguments about money can dim the pleasure you deserve to have with your beloved. Discuss with your mate how you both think your money should be spent. If you can both agree on a budget, your life together will be more mutually satisfying.

FINANCES

House and riches are the inheritance of fathers: and a prudent wife is from the LORD.

PROVERBS 19:14

Learning to Love

Loving sex binds a marriage together. Love your spouse unconditionally. Without reserve. Don't use sex as a reward for good behavior or as a threat to get what you want. Love each other abundantly and well.

SEX

The wife hath not power of her own body, but the husband: and likewise also the husband hath not power of his own body, but the wife.

1 CORINTHIANS 7:4

Learning to Love

Seek harmony in your relationship with your loved one. Don't take detours to total agreement. Talk about your differences until there is full understanding. Do not be afraid of a healthy compromise. Live with your beloved in peace.

ONE MIND

Be perfect, be of good comfort, be of one mind, live in peace; and the God of love and peace shall be with you.

2 CORINTHIANS 13:11

21

Learning to Love

Good judgment helps pave
the way to a lasting and whole
relationship with the one you
love. Seek wisdom as you live
your lives together. If you lack
wisdom, ask of God and He
will supply your need.

JUDGMENT

*And this I pray, that your love
may abound yet more and more
in knowledge and in all judgment.*

PHILIPPIANS 1:9

Learning to Love

Love has a sweet savor. Enjoy
the essence of the love you
share. Be extravagant often
and give yourselves perfumes
and ointments that delight
the senses. Rejoice in the
love of your hearts.

SAVOR

Ointment and perfume rejoice
the heart. . . .

PROVERBS 27:9

Learning to Love

Make love to your spouse
with abandon. God has given
you marriage for pleasure as
well as for family ties. Enjoy
your nights together as much
as you cherish your days.

LOVEMAKING

*Marriage is honorable in all,
and the bed undefiled. . . .*

HEBREWS 13:4

Learning to Love

Do not yield to the temptation
to take another into your
arms. Adultery may seem a
pleasant diversion, but the
end result can be the death
of a marriage. Be true to the
one you love and relish your
mate's uniqueness and beauty.

LUST

*But every man is tempted, when
he is drawn away of his own lust,
and enticed. Then when lust hath
conceived, it bringeth forth sin;
and sin, when it is finished,
bringeth forth death.*

JAMES 1:14, 15

Learning to Love

Put actions behind your sweet
words of love. Don't just say
"I love you," show your beloved
how much you care. Look for
things you can do to please
your mate—*every day*.

ACTIONS

*My little children, let us not love
in word, neither in tongue; but in
deed and in truth.*

1 JOHN 3:18

Learning to Love

God is the One who joined you together with your beloved. He is the one who ordained marriage between a man and a woman. If you need guidance in your marriage—and you will—ask it from the One who abundantly and freely gives.

BONDED

For this cause shall a man leave father and mother, and shall cleave to his wife. . . . What therefore God hath joined together, let not man put asunder.

MATTHEW 19:5, 6

Learning to Love

Be patient in your love.
Don't insist on returning
a harsh word that has been
spoken. Don't always try to
make the last parting shot
in an argument. Love your
spouse even when your mate
is not acting in love.

AFFECTION

*For if ye love them which love you,
what reward have ye? do not even
the publicans the same? Be ye therefore perfect, even as your Father
which is in heaven is perfect.*

MATTHEW 5:46, 48

Learning to Love

If you feel you need strength
to continue to love your
mate, don't despair. God has
promised to give His all
encompassing strength to
those who ask it of Him. So be
patient and prayerfully wait.

UPLIFT

*Wait on the LORD: be of good
courage, and he shall strengthen thine
heart: wait, I say, on the LORD.*

PSALM 27:14

Learning to Love

Guard your heart against the possibility of an adulterous affair. Don't even fantasize about having an affair. The fantasy is the first step toward a reality that could destroy your marriage.

FANTASY

Ye have heard that it was said by them of old time, Thou shalt not commit adultery: but I say unto you, That whosoever looketh on a woman to lust after her hath committed adultery with her already in his heart.

MATTHEW 5:27, 28

Learning to Love

Develop godlike patterns in
your life with your beloved.
Ask yourself how God would
like you to treat your mate.
Never settle for less. Be kind,
be patient, be filled with a
loving mercy.

PATTERNS

Be ye therefore merciful, as your
Father also is merciful.

LUKE 6:36

Learning to Love

A spouse's conversation can be like the sound of constant dripping water—nagging and irritating. Or it can gladden the heart like a bubbling stream. Let your words be ever pleasant.

CONVERSATION

Likewise, ye wives, be in subjection to your own husbands; that, if any obey not the word, they also may without the word be won by the conversation of the wives.

1 PETER 3:1

Growing Together

God crowns each year of
our life with His goodness.
His mercy and love cushion
us from life's hard blows. His
care goes before us, and He
prepares a way for us
through all our days.

GOODNESS

*Thou crownest the year with thy
goodness; and thy paths drop fatness.*

PSALM 65:11

Growing Together

As a new day begins, remember
God has brought you and your
loved one together for a life
of joy and fruitfulness.
Don't settle for less.

FRUITFULNESS

*They shall still bring forth fruit in old
age; they shall be fat and flourishing.*

PSALM 92:14

Growing Together

Thank God for your friends
and family. The bonds of love
that draw you to each other
are blessed by God. He wants
you to rejoice in the ties of
love He has given you.

FAMILIES

*God setteth the solitary in families:
he bringeth out those which are
bound with chains: but the
rebellious dwell in a dry land.*

PSALM 68:6

Growing Together

Prayer cements your heart
to the heart of your beloved.
Take time to pray with the
special one you love. In
praying, you draw near to
the soul of the one who
means so much to you.

PRAYER

*For where two or three are gathered
together in my name, there am
I in the midst of them.*

MATTHEW 18:20

Growing Together

Love has its price. When you
stand with your beloved, you
can not always stand with
the rest of the world. But it
is the willingness to make
this choice that is a sign
of true love.

CHOICES

*Therefore shall a man leave his father
and his mother, and shall cleave unto
his wife: and they shall be one flesh.*

GENESIS 2:24

Growing Together

Embrace your beloved with a joyful heart. Be happy and delight in the smile, the kiss, and the love of the one who rules your heart. Let your joy shine in your eyes and be evident in the words of your mouth.

JOYFUL

Let the field be joyful, and all that is therein: then shall all the trees of the wood rejoice.

PSALM 96:12

Growing Together

Your love grows from a seed
that God planted in your
heart. No one succeeds in
truly loving another unless
God gives him or her the
ability. It's God who makes
your love flourish. Remember
Him in worship and prayer.

SEED

*Those that be planted in the house
of the Lord shall flourish in the
courts of our God.*

PSALM 92:13

Growing Together

Lying in bed with your loved one keeps you warm through all of life's seasons. When you are together in your intimacy, you can forget the storms that rage outside. So draw near to each other and be warm.

WARMTH

Again, if two lie together, then they have heat: but how can one be warm alone?

ECCLESIASTES 4:11

Growing Together

You and your beloved both grow as you seek to know God better. Don't be content with a glimpse of Him. Search the Scriptures and yearn to see His face clearly. He'll show Himself to those who seek Him.

SEEK

Seek the LORD, and his strength: seek his face evermore.

PSALM 105:4

Growing Together

God promises you peace as you draw near to Him. When you are bitter or angry, don't keep your feelings to yourself. Talk about them with a friend. Then bring your concerns to a God who loves you. He will give you peace.

PEACE

Great peace have they which love thy law: and nothing shall offend them.

PSALM 119:165

Growing Together

Share your troubles with your beloved. Together you can work to turn your troubles into triumphs. No one is able to do alone what two can do together, especially when it comes to prayer.

SHARING

And Isaac intreated with the LORD for his wife, because she was barren: and the LORD was intreated of him, and Rebekah his wife conceived.

GENESIS 25:21

Growing Together

Don't neglect the reading of
God's Word with your
beloved. Spending time
together getting to know God
better is one of the richest joys
you will know as a couple.
His Word will delight and
strengthen you.

SCRIPTURE

*Thy word is very pure: therefore
thy servant loveth it.*

PSALM 119:140

Growing Together

God blesses the pleasure you
share with the one you have
married. Savor the sweetness
of sleeping in your beloved's
arms. Carry the sweetness
into the day; let it be a
comfort to you.

PLEASURE

*A bundle of myrrh is my
well-beloved unto me; he shall lie
all night betwixt my breasts.*

SONG OF SOLOMON 1:13

Growing Together

God made you to love and be
loved by those of the opposite
sex, from your parent to
teenage friends to the one
who has become your mate.
Rejoice in the maleness of
men and the femaleness
of women.

CREATED

*From the beginning of the creation
God made them male and female.*

MARK 10:6

Growing Together

One of the joys and mysteries of life is the way in which a man and a woman can become one. The two come together physically, emotionally, and spiritually. They are no longer two: they are one.

ONE

And they twain shall be one flesh: so then they are no more twain, but one flesh.

MARK 10:8

Growing Together

Uncontrollable anger can destroy love. Learn to make your anger a tool to resolve problems rather than let it become a problem itself. Don't let anger build inside until you explode. Handle each day's disagreements that day.

DISAGREEMENTS

He that is slow to anger is better than the mighty; and he that ruleth his spirit than he that taketh a city.

PROVERBS 16:32

Growing Together

Power and love—how do they mix? Each couple needs to pray and consider how they are to relate to one another. Without love, power is harsh. When there is love, there is no need for power.

POWER

But I would have you know, that the head of every man is Christ; and the head of the woman is the man; and the head of Christ is God.

1 CORINTHIANS 11:3

Growing Together

Love doesn't stay the same.
It shrinks and it expands.
Encourage love to grow so
that the love you share with
your mate tomorrow, next
month, or next year is larger
and greater than the love
you share today.

MULTIPLY

*Mercy unto you, and peace,
and love, be multiplied.*

JUDE 2

Growing Together

God made wedding vows as
strong as steel and as fragile
as cut glass. Protect and honor
the promises you've made to
your beloved. Don't let anyone
come between you and
your spouse.

JOINED

*What therefore God hath joined
together, let not man put asunder.*

MARK 10:9

Growing Together

Learn to hold your loved
one tightly. Don't take the one
you love for granted. Tell your
beloved of your feelings.
Love is a precious gift and
needs to be cherished.
Say "I love you" today.

CLEAVE

*For this cause shall a man leave
his father and mother, and cleave
to his wife.*

MARK 10:7

Growing Together

When others criticize your
beloved, don't join in. Be
supportive of your mate.
Temper any of your own
criticisms with the solid
assurance that you are
on your lover's side.

CRITICS

*And if one prevail against him,
two shall withstand him. . . .*

ECCLESIASTES 4:12

Growing Together

Love your mate abundantly.
Be generous and tell your
beloved often of your love.
Tell others that you love
this special person. Let love
shine in your eyes and be
demonstrated in your words.

BANNER

*He brought me to the banqueting
house, and his banner over
me was love.*

SONG OF SOLOMON 2:4

Growing Together

As you grow to know your beloved, grow also to know the Lord who watches over both of you. Spend time meditating on the Word of God. Do not be content with only a surface knowledge of the Savior. Dig deeply into the riches of His presence.

SATISFIED

As for me, I will behold thy face in righteousness; I shall be satisfied when I awake, with thy likeness.

PSALM 17:15

Growing Together

If you have made a major mistake in your relationship with your beloved, don't despair. Be thankful, it's always possible to begin anew. Ask your mate for forgiveness and a clean slate. With God's help, you can and will enjoy an even more fruitful and satisfying life together.

RENEWAL

Create in me a clean heart, O God; and renew a right spirit within me.

PSALM 51:10

Growing Together

Speak honestly to your mate.
Don't be politely silent when
hurt and anger pulse through
your veins. Honest words
spoken in love make your
relationship grow and flourish.

HONESTY

*The words of his mouth were
smoother than butter, but war was
in his heart; his words were softer
than oil, yet were they drawn swords.*

PSALM 55:21

Growing Together

Take time to enjoy your
beloved. Refresh your spirit
and your love with time
together in a quiet, special
place. Forget your troubles
for a moment and speak
only of the love you share.

EACH OTHER

*As the apple tree among the trees of
the wood, so is my beloved among
the sons. I sat down under his shadow
with great delight, and his fruit was
sweet to my taste.*

SONG OF SOLOMON 2:3

Growing Together

Don't try to hold your marriage together by yourself. Ask God for His grace and mercy on your union. God specializes in healing broken hearts. He brings His oil of love and kindness to households where peace is in short supply.

MERCY

But I am like a green olive tree in the house of God: I trust in the mercy of God for ever and ever.

PSALM 52:8

Growing Together

Love draws you close to your
beloved until the lines that
separate you grow indistinct.
God's Word says that marriage
vows bring people together
until they are flesh of the
same flesh and bone of
the same bone.

FLESH

*And Adam said, "This is now bone
of my bones, and flesh of my flesh:
she shall be called Woman, because
she was taken out of Man."*

GENESIS 2:23

Growing Together

Riches do not bring happiness.
Finding peace with your
beloved will. Expensive
presents will never make up
for unloving actions. Learn
to love with your actions,
not just with your wallet or
purse alone.

HANDS FILLED

Better is a handful with quietness,
than both the hands full with travail
and vexation of spirit.

ECCLESIASTES 4:6

Growing Together

Love's first breath can be
sweet. But true love grows
with the years until the first
part of love is only a shadow
of the real tie that binds
a couple together after a
lifetime of love.

ENDINGS

*Better is the end of a thing than
the beginning thereof: and the
patient in spirit is better than
the proud in spirit.*

ECCLESIASTES 7:8

Comforting Each Other

You don't need to bear your troubles alone. Speak openly to your beloved about the deepest concerns of your heart. Then together go to God in prayer, asking Him to lift your burden and ease your anxiety. Let a gracious and loving Savior help you with your every challenge.

TOGETHER

Cast thy burden upon the LORD, and he shall sustain thee. . . .

PSALM 55:22

Comforting Each Other

Hold your mate tightly when trouble enters your relationship and begins to shake your lives. Don't be afraid to cry. God made you and your emotions and put them into one body called YOU! Tears cleanse. God wants you to tell Him how you feel so He can provide for you the comfort He promises.

MOURN

Blessed are they that mourn:
for they shall be comforted.

MATTHEW 5:4

Comforting Each Other

Don't comfort your beloved
from a standpoint of weakness.
Be strong. Have courage. Speak
the truth in love. Comfort
your spouse in a way that
brings encouragement. Help
build on strengths that already
exist. Remember, life has
many seasons, and troubles
come and go. You always have
reason to hope.

ENCOURAGEMENT

*Wherefore comfort yourselves
together, and edify one another,
even as also ye do.*

1 THESSALONIANS 5:11

Comforting Each Other

God doesn't ask you to have
blind trust in Him. He knows
your troubles and that their
pain often overwhelms you.
That's why He offers you and
your beloved a refuge, an
ever-present haven during the
stormy times. Come to Him
together in prayer and let
Him give you the delight of
His own heart.

REFUGE

Trust in him at all times; ye people,
pour out your heart before him:
God is a refuge for us.

PSALM 62:8

Comforting Each Other

Don't give up hope when the
dreams you have for you and
your beloved seem to be
impossible. God specializes
in making the impossible
possible. He enjoys helping
you make your dreams come
true. Talk to Him about what is
on your heart. Do it now.

IMPOSSIBLE

*And Jesus looking upon them saith,
"With men it is impossible, but not
with God: for with God all
things are possible."*

MARK 10:27

Comforting Each Other

When you find it difficult to
be patient because of conflicts
with your mate, remember
God has asked you to maintain
your love relationship in spite
of these challenges. Be patient
and help ease the troubles of
the one you love.

SUBMISSION

*Wives, submit yourselves unto your
own husbands, as unto the Lord. . . .
Husbands, love your wives, even
as Christ also loved the church,
and gave himself for it.*

EPHESIANS 5:22, 25

Comforting Each Other

Comfort your beloved with
words of understanding and
cheer. Don't focus your
conversation on your troubles.
God loves a cheerful heart,
and so will the one you love.

CHEER

*Heaviness in the heart of man
maketh it stoop: but a good
word maketh it glad.*

PROVERBS 12:25

Comforting Each Other

When you are feeling sad, take a few moments to remember how God has worked in the life of you and your beloved in the past. Take comfort from the past successes you have enjoyed together.

THE PAST

I remembered thy judgments of old, O LORD; and have comforted myself.

PSALM 119:52

Comforting Each Other

You never need to fix
the pieces of a broken heart
alone. Take your sadness to
friends and especially to that
friend who sticks closer than
a brother, Jesus Christ. He
promises to heal the wounds
of those who call Him Lord.

HEALING

*The LORD is nigh unto them that
are of a broken heart. . . .*

PSALM 34:18

71

Comforting Each Other

When you feel inadequate to
ease the pain of your beloved,
remember God is the One
who heals the body and the
spirit. Bring your beloved to
Him in earnest prayer. God is
faithful and promises to listen
to your most desperate plea.

INADEQUATE

*For a certain woman, whose young
daughter had an unclean spirit,
heard of him, and came and fell
at his feet. . . . And when she was
come to her house, she found the
devil gone out, and her daughter
laid upon the bed.*

MARK 7:25, 30

Comforting Each Other

Every marriage has its ups and downs. No man or woman has ever been perfect in love. As you recognize your own humanity, ask God to take the hurts in your relationship and show you and your beloved how to turn your challenges into triumphs.

GLADNESS

Thou hast turned for me my mourning into dancing: thou hast put off my sackcloth, and girded me with gladness.

PSALM 30:11

Comforting Each Other

Hold your spouse closely
when you face grief together.
Weep together over your
losses. But remember that
God is able to turn your
night of darkness into a
wonderful, fulfilling
morning of light and joy.

MORNING

Weeping may endure for a night,
but joy cometh in the morning.

PSALM 30:5

Comforting Each Other

The death of a loving parent can shake you and your beloved to your core. It may be extremely difficult to accept this great loss. However, as you and your spouse grieve together, be thankful to a merciful God that He has given you someone to share your deepest pain.

DEATH

And Isaac brought her into his mother Sarah's tent, and took Rebekah, and she became his wife; and he loved her: and Isaac was comforted after his mother's death.

GENESIS 24:67

Comforting Each Other

Sometimes the heartaches in your life will seem too much to bear. But never forget that you and your mate have a special hiding place. The Word of God promises you that your heavenly Father comforts and hides His children under His wings.

HIDING

Keep me as the apple of the eye; hide me under the shadow of thy wings.

PSALM 17:8

Comforting Each Other

God never said He would take away all your burdens. You and your beloved will both struggle until the day you die. That is simply life! But God has promised to make your burdens lighter, never to give you more than you can bear, and to give you His divine rest as you carry them.

REST

Come unto me, all ye that labor and are heavy laden, and I will give you rest.

MATTHEW 11:28

Comforting Each Other

Sometimes you will have to do things that may frighten you. Perhaps you'll need to change jobs, move to a new city, or move out of your "comfort zone" to take on a brand new challenge. Be brave and live today and always in the awareness that you can be confident God goes before you and will give you the strength you need.

BRAVERY

Be of good courage, and he shall strengthen your heart, all ye that hope in the LORD.

PSALM 31:24

Comforting Each Other

As you and your beloved grow to maturity, you will see that it was during the really *tough times* that you developed your stability, resolve, and inner strength. Be comforted in your troubles, because that is one way in which an all-knowing God shapes and perfects you.

MATURITY

Now no chastening for tbe present seemeth to be joyous, but grievous: nevertheless, afterward it yieldeth the peaceable fruit of righteousness unto them which are exercised thereby.

HEBREWS 12:11

Comforting Each Other

Don't just count on seeing
God's fair treatment in heaven.
The Psalmist says God works
justice in our earthly lives as
well. In the *here and now!* Ask
a just and loving God to work
in your life and to keep you
faithful to Him at all times.
Whatever the cost.

FAIR TREATMENT

*I had fainted, unless I had believed
to see the goodness of the LORD
in the land of the living.*

PSALM 27:13

Comforting Each Other

In the stress and challenges
of life, sometimes you may
forget that your presence is a
comfort to your mate. Make
it a point to be with your
beloved when you know your
loved one is going through
difficult times.

HOME

When a man hath taken a new wife,
he shall not go out to war, neither
shall he be charged with any business;
but he shall be free at home one
year, and shall cheer up his wife
which he hath taken.

DEUTERONOMY 24:5

Comforting Each Other

It's a physical law—your life is going to be filled with alterations both good and bad. God is able to work in every circumstance of your life. Sadness may be for a night but joy, fulfillment, and comfort will visit you in the morning.

ALTERATION

To every thing there is a season, and a time to every purpose under the heaven: . . . a time to embrace, and a time to refrain from embracing, a time to get, and a time to lose. . . .

ECCLESIASTES 3:1, 5, 6

Comforting Each Other

At times you may wonder if God is either sleeping or dead. Well, don't despair. The Psalmist reminds us that God never sleeps nor slumbers. He is always awake, attentive, and aware of the trials that you face. Start trusting Him in a new way. Start today!

WATCHFUL

He will not suffer thy foot to be moved: he that keepeth thee will not slumber.

PSALM 121:3

Comforting Each Other

Don't worry about your daily
needs. God watches over all
His creation, and He sees and
knows what is vital for your
sustenance. Come to Him with
your beloved and tell Him
what you need each day.
Come to Him in faith—
believing He will do
what He promises.

NEEDS

*Wherefore, if God so clothe the grass
of the field, which today is, and
tomorrow is cast into the oven, shall
he not much more clothe you,
O ye of little faith?*

MATTHEW 6:30

Comforting Each Other

Sometimes you may feel like God is far away from you and the ones you hold dear. But in reality, God is near at hand no matter where you are— from the top of the highest mountain to the bottom of the deepest ocean.

CLOSER

If I take the wings of the morning, and dwell in the uttermost parts of the sea; even there shall thy hand lead me, and thy right hand shall hold me.

PSALM 139:9, 10

Comforting Each Other

When you are unhappy,
imagine yourself being held
tightly in the arms of God
your Father. Sometimes you
must travel deep into the
valley of tears before you
can begin to scale the great
mountain of joy. Remember,
unhappiness does not
last forever.

TEARS

*They that sow in tears
shall reap in joy.*

PSALM 126:5

Comforting Each Other

New life arises out of sorrow.
As you comfort yourself and
your beloved, think about
how you can redeem your
hard times. Learn to bring
good out of what for the
moment seems bad. Like the
apostle Paul, be content in
whatever circumstances
you and your spouse
find yourselves.

REDEEM

*And David comforted Bathsheba his
wife, and went in unto her, and lay
with her: and she bare a son, and
he called his name Solomon:
and the LORD loved him.*

2 SAMUEL 12:24

Comforting Each Other

Throughout history people
have asked God, "Why, Lord,
why?" You are not alone if you
find yourself asking this
question. Be bold—ask God
to give you understanding of
His deepest mysteries.

WHY?

That their hearts might be comforted,
being knit together in love, and
unto all riches of the full assurance of
understanding, to the acknowledgement
of the mystery of God, and of the
Father, and of Christ.

COLOSSIANS 2:2

Comforting Each Other

Loneliness can weigh heavily
when you face a difficult
decision. If you and your mate
cannot agree on the path you
are about to take, agree to
disagree without pulling
away from each other.

AGREEMENT

Reproach hath broken my heart;
and I am full of heaviness: and
I looked for some to take pity, but
there was none; and for comforters,
but I found none.

PSALM 69:20

Comforting Each Other

Be fierce in your loyalty to your mate. Don't let others belittle the one you love. Show your beloved that you can be counted on no matter what situations arise.

PRESENCE

So Jonathan arose from the table in fierce anger, and did eat no meat the second day of the month: for he was grieved for David, because his father had done him shame.

1 SAMUEL 20:34

Comforting Each Other

God promises you and your beloved a safe dwelling place in Him. Bring your hurts and disappointments to your loving Father who wants only His best for you. Don't try to face life on your own. Live your life by living and loving *together*.

SAFETY

But whoso hearkeneth unto me shall dwell safely, and shall be quiet from fear of evil.

PROVERBS 1:33

Comforting Each Other

Grief and loss come to all of us. You and your spouse are no exception. When you sense your life is empty and you are discouraged, talk with God—and with your mate—about how you feel and discuss how you can rise above the circumstances and meet life head-on with joy and enthusiasm.

DISCOURAGEMENT

I am weary of my crying: my throat is dried: mine eyes fail while I wait for my God.

PSALM 69:3

Comforting Each Other

Say "I love you" often to your
spouse. Many hearts have
grown dry waiting to hear
those three precious words.
Say them often with deep
feeling, and they will make
your relationship a refreshing
oasis in the desert.

REFRESHMENT

Repent ye therefore, and be converted,
that your sins may be blotted out,
when the times of refreshing shall
come from the presence of the Lord.

ACTS 3:19

Accepting One Another

Love captivates the beloved
and holds with soft bonds
of affection. Thoughts of
personal desires and freedom
pale beside the promise
of plunging to the depths of
another's heart and spirit.
This is what true, self-giving
love is all about.

CAPTIVATES

*I am my beloved's,
and my beloved is mine.*

SONG OF SOLOMON 6:3

Accepting One Another

Resentment and unresolved
anger slice through love.
They afflict wounds that may
take a lifetime of recovery.
Give up those grudges that
may one day turn to cold
anger. Tell your beloved how
you feel, and seek to live
together in peace.

PEACE

*The LORD will bless
his people with peace.*

PSALM 29:11

Accepting One Another

Trust is built when two people
keep and cherish each other's
secrets. Protect your beloved's
privacy with the same care
you use to guard your own.
Show your faithfulness to
your mate in this manner.

PRIVACY

*A talebearer revealeth secrets:
but he that is of a faithful spirit
concealeth the matter.*

PROVERBS 11:13

Accepting One Another

True love doesn't keep score
of the wrongs of another.
If you continue to tally the
wrongs of your beloved and
refuse to let go of the past,
you simply cannot grow into
a relationship filled with grace
and forgiveness. Forgive and
forget. You will both be the
winners in the long run.

WRONGS

*If thou, LORD, shouldest mark
iniquities, O Lord, who shall stand?
But there is forgiveness with thee.*

PSALM 130:3, 4

Accepting One Another

True love must stretch when
personal growth begins to
take place. Give your beloved
room to be God's whole,
complete person. Be an
encouragement and not a
discouragement. Recognize
that *change* is an important
part of development.

CHANGE

Charity suffereth long, and is kind;
charity envieth not; charity vaunteth
not itself; is not puffed up.

1 CORINTHIANS 13:4

Accepting One Another

God is the judge of your
actions. He will either reward
or discipline you for your
deeds. Don't waste time acting
as judge, jury, and executioner
of your beloved's actions.
God will deliver His own
justice to all people. Your task
is to love, listen, and care
for the one you love.

JUSTICE

*But God is the judge: he putteth
down one, and setteth up another.*

PSALM 75:7

Accepting One Another

Love is the balm that eases
the friction of life between
two people who have made
a lifelong commitment to
each other. You and your
spouse are not the same.
That's what drew you together
in the first place. Don't let
irritation spoil the pleasure
you have with your beloved.
Apply the healing balm
of love often. Start right now.

IRRITATION

*Hatred stirreth up strifes:
but love covereth all sins.*

PROVERBS 10:12

Accepting One Another

Truth is a precious gift.
It's yours for the taking.
Telling the truth is the key to
being known by each other
and feeling the wonder of
being wholly approved of
by your beloved.

APPROVAL

Charity . . . rejoiceth not in iniquity,
but rejoiceth in the truth;

1 CORINTHIANS 13:4, 6

Accepting One Another

Your words of love are of
more value than the costliest
pearls. Give love words freely
to your beloved. Don't let a
lack of self-confidence or
doubt rob you of the joy of
sharing expressions of
romance and affection.

VALUE

*Even a fool, when be holdeth
his peace, is counted wise: and he
that shutteth his lips is esteemed
a man of understanding.*

PROVERBS 17:28

Accepting One Another

Weave kindness through
the fabric of your love.
This thread must be strong
enough to hold the more
fragile emotions together.
Seek to be kind to your mate.
Look for special ways to be
gentle and sensitive. Together
you can weather any storm.

KINDNESS

Be ye kind one to another,
tenderhearted, forgiving one
another, even as God for
Christ's sake hath forgiven you.

EPHESIANS 4:32

Accepting One Another

Unresolved anger opens
wounds and causes pain
to spread throughout the
relationship with your
beloved. Cleanse your wounds
before anger can take over.
Be honest with your feelings.
Anger is based on hurt, fear,
or frustration. Deal with the
real issues—in truth and love.

ANGER

*He that is slow to wrath
is of great understanding.*

PROVERBS 14:29

Accepting One Another

Fill your mind with wondrous
thoughts of the good things
God has given you and your
beloved—the life you share,
the love that draws you to
each other— the faith that
helps you grow.

THOUGHTS

*Finally, brethren, whatsoever things
are true, whatsoever things are
honest, whatsoever things are just,
whatsoever things are pure, whatsoever
things are lovely, whatsoever things
are of good report; if there be any
virtue, and if there be any praise,
think on these things.*

PHILIPPIANS 4:8

Accepting One Another

Love can easily be clouded over with discouragement and despair. Sometimes you will find yourself confused, not knowing which direction to turn for help in your relationship. The good news is that God promises to give you His understanding in all matters. Lean on Him for His mercy and guidance.

UNDERSTANDING

If any of you lack wisdom, let him ask of God, that giveth to all men liberally, and upbraideth not; and it shall be given him.

JAMES 1:5

Accepting One Another

Love is a dance of poetry.
Each lover bows to the other
and says "No, please, you go
first." Bring the poetry of
"you first" back into your
relationship with your
beloved. Outdo each other
showing love one for the
other. It will sweeten your
love and make it stronger.

ESTEEM

*Let nothing be done through strife
or vainglory; but in lowliness of
mind let each esteem other
better than themselves.*

PHILLIPPIANS 2:3

Accepting One Another

You and your beloved stand
naked before your Father in
Heaven, stripped of your
defenses, apologies, and
excuses. He sees—and
miraculously loves—the
real untarnished YOU!
Give thanks for His acceptance.

DEFENSELESS

Above all things have fervent charity
among yourselves: for charity shall
cover the multitude of sins.

1 PETER 4:8

Accepting One Another

God has a cozy place for
you and your spouse in His
fatherly heart. When you are
sad, He invites you to come
to Him and share your every
burden. He will share His heart
with you and give you peace.
Come to Him today and
feel His love.

HEART

*God is love; and he that dwelleth
in love dwelleth in God, and
God in him.*

1 JOHN 4:16

Accepting One Another

Remember the first
recognition of mutual love
you shared with your
beloved—the excitement,
the rush of ecstasy, the tingle
of fear. Rekindle the passion of
those first moments of love.
Treat your spouse as kindly
today as you did on your
first date. You just may be
amazed at the response.

REKINDLE

*As the apple tree among the trees
of the wood, so is my beloved
among the sons.*

SONG OF SOLOMON 2:3

Accepting One Another

Love is wonderfully contagious. God's loving kindness to you can prompt you to acts of loving kindness to your spouse. Let your entire household be infected with the joy of loving. Spread that joy today—wherever you are and whatever you do.

CONTAGIOUS

Beloved, if God so loved us, we ought also to love one another.

1 JOHN 4:11

Accepting One Another

The path of love often leads
through webs of pain and
hope unobserved by others.
Your private fears and dreams
are yours alone until you
share them with that special
one you love. Explore
unseen places gently.

UNSEEN

*The righteous shall be glad in the
LORD, and shall trust in him.*

PSALM 64:10

Accepting One Another

True love has weak eyesight.
Faults are not seen and
imperfections are not noted.
Open your life wide to the
forgiving eyes of your beloved.
Only in openness is knowing
one another possible.

FORGIVING

*For every tree is known
by his own fruit. . . .*

LUKE 6:44

Accepting One Another

Ask God to spread His light
of love around the hearts of
you and your beloved.
His light will be the laser beam
of truth that helps you know
each other in your innermost
being. Such knowing is the
foundation of love.

INNERMOST

*The meek he will guide in judgment:
and the meek will he teach his way.*

PSALM 25:9

Accepting One Another

Woo your beloved with affectionate words and pleasing ways. Drink your mate's refreshing nectar. Seek to know your spouse more deeply every day you share together. Recognize the value of your every moment together. A relationship filled with love makes you a wealthy couple indeed.

BENEFITS

Blessed be the Lord, who daily loadeth us with benefits, even the God of our salvation.

PSALM 68:19

Accepting One Another

God has provided marriage
as one way for His children
to grow to perfection.
When someone knows
you as well as your spouse,
you can always run . . . *but you
can never hide!* Use your learning
about one another to
encourage growth.

PERFECTION

*Wherefore, beloved, seeing that ye
look for such things, be diligent that
ye may be found of him in peace,
without spot, and blameless.*

2 PETER 3:14

Accepting One Another

Troubles can steal the seeds of your marital happiness before you can plant them. Fight the troubles. Store the seeds well. Together with your mate, ask God to help you overcome all your difficulties. He is faithful to grant you His counsel and wisdom. Take advantage of it.

FIGHT

Now the God of hope fill you with all joy and peace in believing, that ye may abound in hope. . . .

ROMANS 15:13

Accepting One Another

Love is a powerful persuader
and seducer. Use your love to
draw your mate closer to the
heart of the one true God.
Guard your own faith so your
mate does not entice you
away from Him.

ENTICEMENT

*Abstain from fleshly lusts, which
war against the soul; having your
conversation honest . . . that they
may by your good works . . .
glorify God. . . .*

1 PETER 2:12

Accepting One Another

Build your marriage upon the sure foundation of a shared faith and hope in the Lord Jesus Christ. If you and your beloved are aiming at the same targets and moving toward the same goals, your opportunities for growth and fulfillment are magnified many times over.

FOUNDATION

Therefore whosoever heareth these sayings of mine, and doeth them, I will liken him unto a wise man, which built his house upon a rock.

MATTHEW 7:24

Accepting One Another

When you lie in your bed
at night, loneliness may
sometimes flood your soul
even though your mate is
lying by your side. See this
as your inner yearning for the
God who promises to fill your
innermost being with joy.

LONGINGS

*My soul breaketh for the longing
that it hath unto thy judgments
at all times.*

PSALM 119:20

Accepting One Another

Sow seeds of righteousness
and joy in your relationship
with your beloved. Cultivate
happiness together. God will
cause the seeds to grow to
full bloom when you make
Him first in your lives.

PLANTING

*For as the earth bringeth forth her
bud, and as the garden causeth the
things that are sown in it to spring
forth; so the Lord GOD will cause
righteousness and praise to spring
forth before all the nations.*

ISAIAH 61:11

Accepting One Another

Enjoy all of life with your
beloved. Walk together on
a balmy afternoon. Enjoy a
stroll in the gentle rain. Put the
cares of business aside and
make a date with your spouse
today. After all, your beloved
is the most important
person in your life.

NATURE

The flowers appear on the earth;
the time of the singing of birds
is come, and the voice of the
turtle is heard in our land.

SONG OF SOLOMON 2:12

Accepting One Another

Try to look at yourself clearly.
God has given you a multitude
of gifts and talents. He has
given perhaps similar—
and perhaps much different—
talents to your mate.
Encourage each other to
develop all the talents God
has given you. Do the best
with what you have.

TALENT

But every man hath his proper
gift of God, one after this manner,
and another after that.

1 CORINTHIANS 7:7

Being Companions

Love has many dimensions
and can make you more
scattered or more centered.
Concentrate and seek to be
of one mind with your mate.
Discuss what you both want
from your relationship and
then pull together to
reach that goal.

CONCENTRATE

*Finally, be ye all of one mind, having
compassion one of another; love
as brethren, be pitiful, be courteous.*

1 PETER 3:8

Being Companions

Your love relationship
orbits around God even as
the moon moves around
the earth. God keeps your
relationship moving, fluid, and
dynamic. Always remember
that your heavenly Father is
the One behind all the love
you give and receive.

MOVEMENT

For thou, O God, hast proved us:
thou hast tried us, as silver is tried.

PSALM 66:10

Being Companions

Savor the companionship
you share with your beloved.
Breathe deeply of the beautiful
fragrance of your love.
Rejoice in the blessings
you enjoy as a couple.

REJOICE

*Let thy fountain be blessed:
and rejoice with the wife of thy youth.*

PROVERBS 5:18

Being Companions

The first taste of love can
strike you like a thunderbolt.
But it's the steady, constant
companionship and friendship
that makes that first
exhaustive moment of passion
grow into a love that
endures for a lifetime.
Grow with your beloved.

INCREASE

*And the Lord make you to
increase and abound in love
one toward another.*

1 THESSALONIANS 3:12

Being Companions

You and your beloved are
intertwined. The love you
have for each other shines all
around you—and the world
smiles at your devotion.
Keep your love shining.
Never betray the love you
share with your mate.

BETRAYAL

*A virtuous woman is a crown
to her husband: but she that
maketh ashamed is as rottenness
in his bones.*

PROVERBS 12:4

Being Companions

Deep in the soul of every
man and woman is the desire
to know God and experience
His divine love. Honor that
desire in your mate and
make God the cornerstone
of your marriage.

SALVATION

*Let all those that seek thee rejoice
and be glad in thee: and let such as
love thy salvation say continually,
Let God be magnified.*

PSALM 70:4

Being Companions

Live in the heart of your
beloved. Risk romance with
the one you love. Speak
the poetry of your love even
if the words don't seem like
polished gems to you. Your
lover will treasure the words.

ROMANCE

*Then she said, "Let me find favor
in thy sight, my lord; for that thou
hast comforted me, and for that
thou hast spoken friendly unto thine
handmaid, though I be not like
unto one of thine handmaidens."*

RUTH 2:13

Being Companions

God sees the hidden heart
of everyone. Give your
innermost thoughts to God
in prayer. Let Him help you
and your mate separate the
good from the bad that you
might be more fruitful for Him.

SEPARATION

*The LORD looked down from
heaven upon the children of men,
to see if there were any that did
understand, and seek God.*

PSALM 14:2

Being Companions

Cry out to God when you feel
lonely. Loneliness can engulf
you and leave you floating
on an endless sea of despair.
Ask God to bring you comfort
and trust Him to help you.

CRY

*Lover and friend hast thou put
far from me, and mine acquaintance
into darkness.*

PSALM 88:18

Being Companions

Love has many faces. Its most
beautiful countenance is the
face of friendship. Cultivate
a deep, lasting friendship with
your beloved. Play together
with abandon, share your
interests, take long walks,
and learn to be of one heart.

FRIENDSHIP

A friend loveth at all times.

PROVERBS 17:17

Being Companions

When you love, your soul
meets and kisses the good
that is inside the soul of your
beloved. Nurture that which is
righteous, correct, and noble
in your beloved . . . and let
your beloved encourage those
same qualities within you.

RIGHTEOUS

Mercy and truth are met together;
righteousness and peace have
kissed each other.

PSALM 85:10

Being Companions

CONFIDENTIAL should be
stamped across your love
relationship in large red letters.
The privacy you give your
beloved makes it possible
to tell of your innermost
thoughts, feeling secure in the
knowledge that they will be
safe with your mate.

CONFIDENTIAL

*He that covereth a transgression
seeketh love; but he that repeateth
a matter separateth very friends.*

PROVERBS 17:9

Being Companions

True love doesn't worry about who's the boss. It doesn't keep score in the "whose turn is it now" game. True love rejoices in doing what is good for the beloved and in serving one another.

SERVANTHOOD

But he that is greatest among you shall be your servant.

MATTHEW 23:11

Being Companions

True love knits two people
together until the threads
of one life are intertwined
with the threads of the other.
Celebrate the unity you share
with your mate. Give thanks
today—right now—by praising
God for what you are
sharing together.

UNITY

Behold, how good and how
pleasant it is for brethren to
dwell together in unity!

PSALM 133:1

Being Companions

Any romantic relationship
falters at times . . . and only
a more mature, wiser person
can tell you how to rekindle
your love. Seek help from
others when you do not know
how to mend a troubled
relationship. Help is near. Be
courageous enough to seek it.

COUNSEL

*Where no counsel is, the people
fall: but in the multitude of
counselors there is safety.*

PROVERBS 11:14

Being Companions

Poets have tried for centuries
to capture the essence of love.
The Bible tells us quite simply
that real love is caring more
about others than you care
for yourself and your own
needs. Be a model of selfless
love in your relationship.
It will be contagious.

LOVE

*Nevertheless, let every one of you
in particular so love his wife even
as himself; and the wife see that
she reverence her husband.*

EPHESIANS 5:33

Being Companions

God has given you and your
mate different skills and
responsibilities. Don't
constantly blame your mate
for things that go wrong.
Ask yourself, "Is some of this
MY responsibility?" Work
together in harmony and
in a spirit of companionship.

BLAME

*In the lips of him that hath
understanding wisdom is found.*

PROVERBS 10:13

Being Companions

What will you do to show your mate how much your love means? Let your beloved know you'd be willing to go to great lengths if necessary. Then put your actions to work to woo your mate all over again. Rekindle your love with a fresh, new commitment.

WINNING

And Jacob loved Rachel; and said, "I will serve thee seven years for Rachel thy younger daughter."

GENESIS 29:18

Being Companions

When metal strikes metal,
both become more finely
honed. The same is true with
two people. Challenge your
beloved—and yourself—
to greater mental thoughts.
Read widely, understand
broadly, push yourself to
greater awareness of the
world around you.

INTELLECT

*Iron sharpeneth iron; so a man
sharpeneth the countenance
of his friend.*

PROVERBS 27:17

Being Companions

Gentleness is like oil that
smooths the friction of
day-to-day living. Gentleness
inspires love and affection.
Be gentle with your mate
as you walk through
your days together.

FRICTION

Let the husband render unto the
wife due benevolence: and likewise
also the wife unto the husband.

1 CORINTHIANS 7:3

Being Companions

Love your mate with your
whole body and soul.
Luxuriate in the delights
of your love. Romance
blooms gently in the midst
of tenderness and
thoughtfulness.
Enjoy the love you share.

WHOLENESS

*I am my beloved's,
and his desire is toward me.*

SONG OF SOLOMON 7:10

Being Companions

Love molds you into many
of the shapes and attitudes of
your beloved. Seek to grow in
positive ways with your mate.
Decide together on what is
important in your lives.
You are two . . . but your
hearts must beat as one.

LIKEMINDED

*Fulfill ye my joy, that ye be
likeminded, having the same love,
being of one accord, of one mind.*

PHILIPPIANS 2:2

Being Companions

Hidden anger and bitterness can turn a love relationship into a cold war. Guard against unresolved anger and learn to talk to your beloved about any hurts or disappointments that arise.

BITTERNESS

Wives, submit yourselves unto your own husbands, as it is fit in the Lord. Husbands, love your wives, and be not bitter against them.

COLOSSIANS 3:18, 19

Being Companions

The vows you took on your wedding day are the most life-changing promises you will ever make. Esteem and honor your vows. Never forsake the love that brought you together.

WEDDING VOWS

For this cause shall a man leave his father and mother, and shall be joined unto his wife, and they two shall be one flesh.

EPHESIANS 5:31

Being Companions

God's hand is the one that
fashioned you and your
beloved—your personalities,
your intellects, your deepest
desires. Rejoice in His presence
in your life together and give
Him your devotion.

DEVOTION

*LORD, thou hast been our dwelling
place in all generations.*

PSALM 90:1

Being Companions

God has promised a dwelling
place for you. When your
life and your relationships
seem dry and unfulfilling,
come to the Lord who loves
you for refreshment and
renewed hope.

DWELLING

Strong is thy dwelling place;
and thou puttest thy nest in a rock.

NUMBERS 24:21

Being Companions

The Father who led Moses
out of the wilderness promises
to lead you to a special
promised land as well. Accept
His guidance and follow His
leading to a place overflowing
with milk and honey.

INHERITANCE

*The seed also of his servants shall
inherit it: and they that love his
name shall dwell therein.*

PSALM 69:36

Being Companions

Arrogance can crush love quicker than almost anything. True love is built on acceptance and kindness one toward another. Protect your relationship with your beloved from the harshness of arrogance.

ARROGANCE

Yea, all of you be subject one to another, and be clothed with humility: for God resisteth the proud, and giveth grace to the humble.

1 PETER 5:5

Being Companions

Rejection can cut through love
like a knife through fine cloth.
If you feel rejected, take your
hurt to God. He knows the
wounds of the rejected and
knows how to heal them.

REJECTION

*He that followeth after
righteousness and mercy findeth
life, righteousness, and honor.*

PROVERBS 21:21

Being Companions

The very core of love is found
in the heart of God. If your
love has grown stale, ask God
to give you an abundance
of the love He so generously
gives to those who ask of
Him. It's still true . . . ASK and
you shall RECEIVE. Accept His
generous offer of love today
for you and your beloved.

ABUNDANCE

*For in him we live, and move,
and have our being.*

ACTS 17:28

Being Companions

A listening heart is a balm
to a damaged relationship. Be
willing to see your relationship
through the eyes of your mate.
God has given you ears
to hear. Ask Him to help
you listen wisely.

LISTEN

*The hearing ear, and the seeing
eye, the LORD hath made even
both of them.*

PROVERBS 20:12

Working Together

The burdens of life may
seem to be impossible. Every
day you observe your own
weaknesses and those of your
beloved. Then you remember
what brought you together
in the first place. You recall that
a couple in love can pull
a heavier load together than
each can pull alone. It's what
commitment to stick together
is all about.

COMMITMENT

*Then shall the earth yield her
increase; and God, even our
own God, shall bless us.*

PSALM 67:6

Working Together

True love is not easily
embarrassed. Seek to help
work out the plan God has
for your beloved's life. Never
allow the teasing or ridicule
of others to ever stop you
from being 100 percent
supportive of your mate.

SUPPORT

*For he that will love life, and see
good days, let him refrain his
tongue from evil, and his lips
that they speak no guile.*

1 PETER 3:10

Working Together

An enduring, loving marriage
is a wondrous monument to
the goodness of a gracious
Lord. As your gray hairs begin
to appear, and your bodies
start to slow down, let your
love for each other increase.
Your life together is your
greatest work for God.

AGING

*Now also when I am old and
grayheaded, O God, forsake me not;
until I have showed thy strength unto
this generation, and thy power
to every one that is to come.*

PSALM 71:18

Working Together

Thank God daily for the
bountiful privileges He has
given to you and your spouse.
Consider what your marriage
and family would be like
if you did not have the
freedoms you are able to
enjoy together. Rejoice in
God's blessings. Be thankful
for your liberty today as you
bring to mind our country's
independence.

FREEDOM

*His seed shall be mighty upon
earth: the generation of the
upright shall be blessed.*

PSALM 112:2

Working Together

Love isn't all hugs and laughter.
Love that's deep and solid also
involves hard work and sweat.
Spend time working with your
beloved. When it's tough, do it
tough. When it's easy, do
it easy. Then take the time
to stand back together and
enjoy the fruits of your
labor together.

LABOR

*Two are better than one; because they
have a good reward for their labor.*

ECCLESIASTES 4:9

Working Together

Our Almighty Father, Ruler
of the heavens and King of all
the earth, wants to bless you
today. Gratefully accept His
love and kind benediction as
you and your beloved go
about your daily tasks.

BENEDICTION

*God be merciful unto us,
and bless us; and cause his face
to shine upon us.*

Working Together

Live so you may look upon
your work and pronounce
it good. Let pride shine in
your face when your labor is
worthy of praise. Give glory to
God for what He has enabled
you and your beloved
mate to accomplish.

PRIDE

*Wherefore I perceive that there is
nothing better, than that a man
should rejoice in his own works;
for that is his portion: for who
shall bring him to see what
shall be after him?*

ECCLESIASTES 3:22

Working Together

Love does not grow by
ironclad rules, seeking to bend
others to its own way. Love
grows in the gentle breeze of
acceptance. Love your mate
closer to your heart with
gentleness, not legislation.

RULES

Love worketh no ill to his neighbor:
therefore love is the fulfilling
of the law.

ROMANS 13:10

Working Together

Not all work is done through
strength. Some of the best
and most enduring work is
accomplished when two
lovers are at the point of
their greatest weakness, both
spiritually and physically.
Don't wait to be strong to do
what God wants you to do.
Simply put your hand to the
task to be done today.

WEAKNESS

*Blessed is the man whose strength
is in thee: in whose heart are the
ways of them.*

PSALM 84:5

Working Together

The best part of love is not
in its intelligence. Love is
notoriously blind. Nor does
the best part lie in its unending
hope. No, the best part of love
is simply in its seeking the
very best for your mate—and
wanting that "best" for your
beloved more than you
desire it for yourself.

BEST

*Charity suffereth long, and is kind;
charity envieth not; charity vaunteth
not itself, is not puffed up.*

1 CORINTHIANS 13:4

Working Together

Make a daily decision that you
and your mate will train your
eyes to behold the workings
of the Lord. Seek to see His
hand in the events around
you. Then give outward thanks
to Him for His help.

WORKINGS

*I will meditate also of all thy work,
and talk of thy doings.*

PSALM 77:12

Working Together

Two hearts don't always
beat as one. However, in the
important matters of your
life together seek harmony
with your mate so you can
experience the joy of life with
agreement and a deep sense
of meaning and purpose.

ACCORD

*Again I say unto you, That if two of
you shall agree on earth as touching
any thing that they shall ask, it
shall be done for them of my
Father which is in heaven.*

MATTHEW 18:19

Working Together

The desire to mate and build a family is given to people from a God who said "be fruitful, multiply, and fill the earth." It is vital that you and your spouse regard your child-rearing years as among the most fulfilling work of your entire lives. You are designing our world's future.

GENERATIONS

Thy seed will I establish for ever, and build up thy throne to all generations.

PSALM 89:4

Working Together

Lie down in repose in the warmth of God's love. His power protects you so you can frolic with your beloved. He smiles when He sees the love that flows between you and your mate in your most tender moments.

PROTECTION

For the LORD God is a sun and shield: the Lord will give grace and glory: no good thing will he withhold from them that walk uprightly.

PSALM 84:11

Working Together

God doesn't stay home in the morning; He goes to work with you. Never forget that He is beside you with each decision and task you need to do during the business day. Ask Him for any wisdom you lack, and He will give it to you from the abundance of a father's heart.

SUBDUED

Is not the LORD your God with you? and hath he not given you rest on every side? for he hath given the inhabitants of the land into mine hand; and the land is subdued before the LORD, and before his people.

1 CHRONICLES 22:18

Working Together

God has made you and your mate as individuals. He gave each of you different talents and abilities. Ask Him how He would like you to use these gifts in His service. Always use your gifts to glorify the Lord!

INDIVIDUALS

Thy hands have made me and fashioned me: give me understanding, that I may learn thy commandments.

PSALM 119:73

Working Together

How do you handle criticism?
How do you respond to
the inadequacies in yourself
and others? Are you sensitive
to the needs and ambitions
of others? Let God teach
you to reflect His love
and understanding
in the workplace.

RESPONSE

*I therefore, the prisoner of the Lord,
beseech you that ye walk worthy of
the vocation wherewith ye are called,
with all lowliness and meekness,
with longsuffering, forbearing one
another in love.*

EPHESIANS 4:1, 2

Working Together

Wisdom from God makes the difference between a successful career and a series of failures. The Bible gives you and your mate a solid foundation for relating justly and honestly to those around you. Ask God for wisdom to build a strong foundation as you work together to make your relationship a success.

CAREER

Teach me good judgment and knowledge: for I have believed thy commandments.

PSALM 119:66

Working Together

Love is a golden thread that
when woven throughout your
days makes your life a beautiful
tapestry for all to see. Don't
ration the love you share with
your mate. Give your love
freely—with reckless abandon.
Let your love be a pleasant
blend of all that is wonderful
and good.

TAPESTRY

*Rest in the LORD, and wait
patiently for him.*

PSALM 37:7

Working Together

Make a pact with your spouse to indulge yourselves with the love of God. God specializes in good gifts. The gift of your mate is but one example of God's boundless care. He has given you a beloved one to love even as He has given Himself generously to you. Stretch your love and let it grow today.

STRETCH

Every good gift and every perfect gift is from above, and cometh down from the Father of lights, with whom is no variableness, neither shadow of turning.

JAMES 1:17

Working Together

As you and your spouse
engage in business, exercise
caution in accepting counsel
from those whose ethics may
be in question. Pick your
counselors and business
associates with great care.
Your reputation, integrity,
and honor are at stake.

ETHICS

*Blessed is the man that walketh not
in the counsel of the ungodly. . . .
He shall be like a tree planted by the
rivers of water, that bringeth forth his
fruit in his season. . . .*

PSALM 1:1–3

Working Together

God created you and your
spouse as natural leaders.
In your workplaces seek
ways to demonstrate your
leadership skills. Encourage
growth in your mate in all
areas of life. If you want to be
a leader—LEAD! Others who
value your guidance will
follow—especially if you
have children.

LEADERSHIP

God created man in his own image . . . ;
male and female created he them.
And God . . . said unto them, Be fruitful,
and multiply, and replenish the earth,
and subdue it: and have dominion
over . . . every living thing that
moveth upon the earth.

GENESIS 1:27–28

Working Together

Honor God with the first
place in your affections.
Give a worthy portion to Him
before you spend liberally on
yourself. Agree with your
spouse to bring the fruits of
your work to God and give
them to Him with devotion.

TITHE

*Honor the LORD with thy substance,
and with the firstfruits of all thine
increase: so shall thy barns be filled
with plenty, and thy presses shall
burst out with new wine.*

PROVERBS 3:9, 10

Working Together

When seeking an occupation,
follow your natural abilities
and desires. God has given
you and your beloved skills
unmatched by others. He
wants you to use them to
His glory. Work diligently as
unto the Lord and He will
bless your labor.

OCCUPATION

Delight thyself also in the LORD;
and he shall give thee the desires
of thine heart.

PSALM 37:4

Working Together

It can be wearisome to
feel all alone in one's work,
especially when the burdens
are heavy. A responsive God
saw the loneliness in man's
heart and made for him a
friend, a companion, a wife.
Enjoy each other to the fullest.
Do something special for
each other today.

WIFE

*And the LORD God said, It is not
good that the man should be alone;
I will make him a help meet for him.*

GENESIS 2:18

Working Together

Some of the most challenging labor in life takes place in the home. It is difficult to be a parent without having someone else to help you in the hard times. Lean on your spouse for support in raising your children.

PARENTING

For if they fall, the one will lift up his fellow: but woe to him that is alone when he falleth; for he hath not another to help him up.

ECCLESIASTES 4:10

Working Together

God has set a standard for
you and your spouse.
Honesty and integrity
are among the two most
important yardsticks He has
created to measure your
performance. Is there anything
that needs improvement?
Talk it over. Listen to each
other. If need be, make
some changes. Start today.

YARDSTICK

For the word of the LORD is right;
and all his works are done in truth.

PSALM 33:4

181

Working Together

Let God's abundance and love
flow through you and your
beloved. God is a generous
rewarder to those who show
mercy and kindness to others.
Find someone needy to love.
Reach out beyond yourselves
in practical kindness.

PRACTICAL

*He that giveth unto the poor
shall not lack.*

PROVERBS 28:27

Working Together

Always give your beloved
verbal credit for a job well
done. Know that God rewards
His children who honestly and
righteously sense Him in the
workplace. Encourage yourself
and your mate through the
difficult times. Be sure to go
out of your way to give
credit where it is due.

CREDIT

Seest thou a man diligent in his
business? He shall stand before kings;
he shall not stand before mean men.

PROVERBS 22:29

Working Together

The Lord gives and the Lord
takes away. God is the one
who controls your destiny
and your days. If you or your
beloved lack anything, go to
the Heavenly Father and ask
Him. He is pleased to provide
for His children.

PROVIDER

Therefore take no thought, saying,
What shall we eat? or What shall
we drink? . . . for your heavenly
Father knoweth that ye have need
of all these things.

MATTHEW 6:31–32

Being Known

Your soul cries out to be known by someone special. And even as you are drawn to a deeper, more intimate relationship with your mate, a loving God chooses to draw you both closer to Himself. Your heavenly Father wants to be known, loved and served. Live in the comfort of knowing your Father cares.

KNOWN

But as for me, my prayer is unto thee, O LORD, in an acceptable time: O God, in the multitude of thy mercy hear me, in the truth of thy salvation.

PSALM 69:13

Being Known

Delight in searching out
the hidden places of your
beloved's mind and soul.
Give your heart to your own
love and to none other. Leave
room for hidden mysteries.

HIDDEN

*Bow down thine ear, and hear the
words of the wise, and apply thine
heart unto my knowledge.*

PROVERBS 22:17

Being Known

Sing softly of your beloved's
virtues. Praise all good things.
Let your pride be seen on your
face. Let your love for your
spouse be a hiding place for
your beloved's imperfections.

IMPERFECTIONS

*And above all these things
put on charity, which is the
bond of perfectness.*

COLOSSIANS 3:14

Being Known

After the sun has set and
darkness covers your face,
seek the sweet communion
of time spent with your
beloved at the merciful throne
of our Father. He will give
you comfort in times of trial
and sustenance when the
challenges seem too great.
Believe in His great
mercy today.

EVENING

*I call to remembrance my song in
the night: I commune with mine
own heart: and my spirit made
diligent search.*

PSALM 77:6

Being Known

Gaze upon the sleeping face of your beloved. When you were courting, words were not enough to describe your mate's inner and outer beauty. Still, you want to know your beloved in greater depth. Keep the exploration alive today and every day. Never be satisfied. Always know there is more to be discovered about your beloved.

SEARCHING

That their hearts might be comforted, being knit together in love. . . .

COLOSSIANS 2:2

Being Known

To some, love comes in a whisper. For others, it arrives with a great tumultuous shout! But from the beginning, words are important. Words either build or destroy. Let your positive, loving speech — coupled with "love actions" — be the proof of your love.

SPEECH

Let your speech be always with grace, seasoned with salt, that ye may know how ye ought to answer every man.

COLOSSIANS 4:6

Being Known

Loving criticism is better than
lying praise. The one purifies
so wounds can heal. The other
encourages infection so that
a temporary peace can be
maintained. Speak the truth
in love with your mate.
Do not shy away from
caring, honest reproof.

CRITICISM

Faithful are the wounds of a friend;
but the kisses of an enemy
are deceitful.

PROVERBS 27:6

Being Known

Wedding days are rapturous and exciting. Congratulations and happy tears abound. But the wedding day ecstasy cannot endure forever. Each 24 hours has its own texture. Appreciate each day for its own value. Like a game of chess, no game or day is ever the same. Enjoy the difference. Appreciate the variety of your love.

APPRECIATE

Say not thou, What is the cause that the former days were better than these? for thou dost not inquire wisely concerning this.

ECCLESIASTES 7:10

Being Known

True politeness is grounded
in considerate truth.
When seeking to know your
beloved, don't be content with
anything less than
straightforward, honest
communication. The roots
of true love grow deeply
when the truth is spoken
with compassion and love.

POLITENESS

*Keep thy tongue from evil,
and thy lips from speaking guile.*

PSALM 34:13

Being Known

Look at the face of your
beloved and you will see
flashes of gold. But, in fact,
what you see is much more
precious than gold. A love
rooted and grounded in
God makes your lover's
countenance shine more
than any earthly treasure.

TREASURE

*For where your treasure is,
there will your heart be also.*

LUKE 12:34

194

Being Known

A love that refuses to show
its face is a worthless love.
Without action and light,
love becomes twisted and
withered. Love needs
acknowledgment to grow to
full force. Let the light of God's
love shine on you and your
mate today and every day as
you continue to stand
together in love.

LIGHT

Open rebuke is better than secret love.

PROVERBS 27:5

Being Known

Hate and love are flip
sides of the same coin.
And sometimes only a coin's
width separates the two.
Love can be wounded so
severely that it loses its value
and deteriorates into hate and
despair. Make both sides of
your coin read "I love you."
Heads you win . . . tails you win too!

HATE

*This is my commandment, that ye
love one another, as I have loved you.*

JOHN 15:12

Being Known

Love is much like an orchestra
responding to the skill and
care of a conductor. No single
instrument can ever be the
sole star. The music and
the harmony of all players
working together is what
makes a thing of beauty.
Live in that kind of harmony
with your spouse. If there is
discord in your heart,
"conduct it out" today.

HARMONY

*Charity . . . doth not behave itself
unseemly, seeketh not her own, is not
easily provoked, thinketh no evil.*

1 CORINTHIANS 13:4–5

197

Being Known

You married because you "fell in love." Now as your love matures you find yourself "standing in love"—an even more mature form of affection. When you truly love you ask, "What can I do for you?" not "What are you going to do for me?"

MARRIED

So ought men to love their wives as their own bodies. He that loveth his wife loveth himself.

EPHESIANS 5:28

Being Known

Priceless pearls are created in
the deep, hidden recesses of
the oyster shell. Let your heart
and soul be as one of those
pearls of great price—quietly
growing in value every day.
Start living this way today!

PEARLS

*Whose adorning, let it not be that
outward adorning . . . but let it be
the hidden man of the heart, in
that which is not corruptible, even
the ornament of a meek and quiet
spirit, which is in the sight of
God of great price.*

1 PETER 3:3–4

Being Known

Your love can be a quiet, flickering candle or a roaring fire. But your true love has flame *only because God has given you the enormous capacity to love.* Thank God for the ability He has freely given to you to share your deepest affection with your beloved.

FLAME

Beloved, let us love one another: for love is of God; and every one that loveth is born of God, and knoweth God.

1 JOHN 4:7

Being Known

Does your love harbor fears?
Will your beloved still love you
if your secrets are known?
Love and acceptance grow
only in the light of the truth.
When you finally share a deep
secret with your mate, do it
with love and care. Shame can
turn to joy when you speak
the truth in love.

SHAME

*But speaking the truth in love . . .
grow up into him in all things,
which is the head, even Christ.*

EPHESIANS 4:15

Being Known

Love is the light that guides
you in your relationship with
your beloved. But your love
isn't perfect. Love can stumble
and cause pain. All that is
required is for you to put the
good of your beloved ahead
of your own desires. If you
stumble, pick yourself up
and start all over again.

STUMBLING

*And let the peace of God rule in your
hearts, to the which also ye are called
in one body; and be thankful.*

COLOSSIANS 3:15

Being Known

Not all of the ways of the Lord
are plain to our earthly eyes.
Sometimes the workings of
the Father are subtle and can
only be observed by the most
discerning mind. Seek to
know how God is working
in the lives of you and
your beloved.

DISCERNMENT

*The secret of the LORD is with them
that fear him; and he will show
them his covenant.*

PSALM 25:14

Being Known

Love makes mistakes. But a willingness to set things right is more important to your beloved than feigned perfection. Talk with your beloved. Two-way communication unearths hidden treasure.

PRETENSE

Who can understand his errors? Cleanse thou me from secret faults.

PSALM 19:12

Being Known

When you share from the
center of your heart, you give
a gift beyond value to your
beloved. Take time to give this
greatest of all treasures.
Share your personal secrets
with your lover alone. True
intimacy will be your reward.

INTIMACY

*When wisdom entereth into the heart,
. . . discretion shall preserve thee,
understanding shall keep thee.*

PROVERBS 2:11

205

Being Known

Courage is the tool that sculpts and refines a loving relationship. It takes courage to tell your beloved that you have been hurt by words or deeds. But do not neglect the cleansing of your hurt feelings. If you do, they will fester and injure your love. Have the courage to speak of your feelings . . . and do it with love in your heart.

COURAGE

Moreover if thy brother shall trespass against thee, go and tell him his fault between thee and him alone.

MATTHEW 18:15

Being Known

Compliments are like a welcome summer breeze after the gales of winter. Tell your beloved of the beauty your eyes see. Speak often of your deep, deep love, and your relationship will blossom. It's still true . . . you will always reap what you sow. Speak love and you harvest love. Let your marriage be a trophy of caring.

BEAUTY

As the lily among thorns, so is my love among the daughters.

SONG OF SOLOMON 2:2

Being Known

Our Father in heaven has given you and your beloved a bountiful marriage. Feast on the delights of your love for each other. Rejoice in the sensations of being joined to your beloved. Feel your love to the edges, and live in the exhilaration of your affection.

SENSATIONS

And they were both naked, the man and his wife, and were not ashamed.

GENESIS 2:25

Being Known

The health of your marriage
rests on the mercy of a loving,
living God. He is the One who
can make the rough ways
smooth and can heal your
broken heart. He steadfastly
gives strength to you—His
child. He is generous, loving,
and kind. Rely on His grace
to keep your marriage
healthy and strong.

GIRDETH

*It is God that girdeth me with strength,
and maketh my way perfect.*

PSALM 18:32

Being Known

True love is spun with the purest of golden thoughts. You dream enchanted dreams of the next time you will be alone with your mate. Strangely and beautifully, time both slows down and speeds up when you are in the presence of your beloved. Keep your love alive in a fresh, creative way. Recapture the wonder of your love.

ENCHANTMENT

And Jacob served seven years for Rachel; and they seemed unto him but a few days, for the love he had to her.

GENESIS 29:20

Being Known

You look into the face of your beloved, searching for a sign of romantic devotion, for a quickly returned glance of adoration. Then you see it in your beloved's eyes—you are well loved. You embrace. You have rediscovered why you are standing in love.

LOOKING

And when Boaz had eaten and drunk, and his heart was merry, he went to lie down at the end of the heap of corn: and she came softly, and uncovered his feet, and laid her down.

RUTH 3:7

Being Known

Wrap yourself in God's holiness. He wants to be your hiding place when you feel sad and forsaken by those who say they love you. He is waiting to comfort and encourage you every day. He will never leave you nor forsake you. That's His promise to you!

FORSAKEN

But thou, O LORD, art a shield for me; my glory, and the lifter up of mine head.

PSALM 3:3

Being Known

Your love relationship is a
place for you to know your
emotions, own your emotions,
and show your emotions. Your
fears, joys, concerns, hurts, and
sky-splitting moments of
ecstasy are all a part of the
person God made you to be.
Celebrate them all with
your beloved.

EMOTIONS

*From the end of the earth will
I cry unto thee, when my heart is
overwhelmed. Lead me to the rock
that is higher than I.*

PSALM 61:2

Being Known

Promises broken and promises kept—these two things both build and destroy trust. Let your words come from your mouth as words that come from your heart. Promise your beloved only what you feel you can deliver.

PROMISES

For thou, O God, hast heard my vows. . . .

PSALM 61:5

Being Known

Comfort is the backbone of
love. Accept your beloved for
who he is. Don't over-correct
your spouse with words of
torment or reproof.
Learn instead to stand beside
your beloved with quiet
encouragement. If you need
to begin this new behavior,
start doing it today.

CORRECTION

*The God of all comfort . . . comforteth
us in all our tribulation, that we
may be able to comfort them
which are in trouble. . . .*

2 CORINTHIANS 1:3–4

Living with Hope

Lift your eyes to the Lord of
the heavens and ask Him to
shower your love relationship
with grace. He is the One who
enables you to love. It is He
who gives you more ability to
love if you ask Him. May His
love encompass you and
your beloved today.

SHOWERS

*He shall come down like rain upon
the mown grass: as showers that
water the earth.*

PSALM 72:6

Living with Hope

Drink your fill of the kisses
of your beloved. Savor the
warmth of your lover's
closeness. God smiles to
see the love you share with
your mate. Rejoice in
your life together.

KISSES

*Let him kiss me with the kisses
of his mouth: for thy love is
better than wine.*

SONG OF SOLOMON 1:2

Living with Hope

When enemies are camped
around you and your beloved,
do not fear. The God who
reigns over all the earth
and heavens will be your
defender and will shield
you from harm.

SHIELD

*Behold, O God our shield, and look
upon the face of thine anointed.*

PSALM 84:9

Living with Hope

Loving someone is not always easy. Everyone has blocks that often stand in the way. Too many times old hurts make us cautious in love. Ask God to continue to bring you to maturity and give you the capacity to love as never before.

CAPACITY

Being confident of this very thing, that he which hath begun a good work in you will perform it until the day of Jesus Christ.

PHILIPPIANS 1:6

Living with Hope

Center your heart around
God, and He will give you
the desires of your heart.
Come to God with your mate
and dedicate your love to
Him. Thank Him for giving
you your life's companion.

CENTER

Rejoice the soul of thy servant:
for unto thee, O Lord, do I lift
up my soul.

PSALM 86:4

Living with Hope

Love your mate with
confidence. Support your
beloved's strengths while
not shying away from the
weaknesses. They are all part
of being human. Believe the
best of your mate even as
you accept the frailness
of your beloved.

ACCEPTANCE

*Charity . . . beareth all things,
believeth all things, hopeth all things,
endureth all things.*

1 CORINTHIANS 13:4–7

Living with Hope

Dance with your love before
the Lord. Be merry in your
affection as you serenade
each other with laughter.
Feel the warm smile of God
upon the lives of you and
your beloved. Celebrate your
togetherness . . . NOW!

MERRY

*Glory ye in his holy name:
let the heart of them rejoice
that seek the LORD.*

PSALM 105:3

Living with Hope

Give the precious gift of your heart to God first and then to your beloved. Do not hold back. Give of yourself freely without counting the price. You'll be rewarded over and over for your efforts.

PRECIOUS

There came unto him a woman having an alabaster box of very precious ointment, and poured it on his head, as he sat at meat.

MATTHEW 26:7

Living with Hope

Love ebbs and flows. If you
are feeling low on affection,
ask God to renew the melody
of love that once sang in your
heart. God is the God of new
beginnings. He will give you
all you ask of Him.

RENEWAL

*Thou sendest forth thy spirit, they
are created: and thou renewest the
face of the earth.*

PSALM 104:30

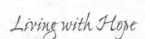

Living with Hope

Let gladness surround your
love and lighten the hearts of
all who see the devotion you
share with your mate. Treat
your beloved like the priceless
treasure that God has shaped
and designed for you.

GLADNESS

*And he brought forth his people with
joy, and his chosen with gladness.*

PSALM 105:43

Living with Hope

A loving heart binds up hurts
with a patient and forgiving
spirit. When you or your
beloved stumble, don't give up
walking toward each other.
Everyone makes mistakes in
love. Remember what drew
you together in the first place.
Have patience and rediscover
each other as the bond you
share stengthens daily.

PATIENCE

*And the Lord direct your hearts
into the love of God, and into the
patient waiting for Christ.*

2 THESSALONIANS 3:5

Living with Hope

God spoke the world into
being. His voice rang out
throughout the universe and
all that lived leapt to obey His
command. Ask God to speak
in your life with your beloved.
Let His love and wisdom be
yours in all your dealings this
day and always.

VOICE

*The voice of the LORD maketh
the hinds to calve, and discovereth
the forests: and in his temple doth
every one speak of his glory.*

PSALM 29:9

Living with Hope

Time belongs to God. Ask Him
to make you a wise steward of
each day He has given you.
Spend time with your spouse
and speak frankly and openly
about the concerns of your
heart. Always make time
for each other.

TIME

*And the LORD appointed a set time,
saying, Tomorrow the LORD shall
do this thing in the land.*

EXODUS 9:5

Living with Hope

Marriage is a great teacher.
You see your own faults more
clearly when placed up against
another's needs. Thank God
for His help as you grow into
the person He wants you to
be. Life is your school, and
your mate is one of your best
teachers. Learn well today
and every day.

LEARNING

The eyes of the Lord are over the
righteous, and his ears are open
unto their prayers.

1 PETER 3:12

Living with Hope

God leads you into pleasant
pastures. Ask Him to bring you
and your beloved to a quiet
oasis where He may give you
a time of rest in your life
together. Focus on your
beloved and confess all the
love that has grown in your
heart thus far.

PLEASANTNESS

*So we thy people and sheep of
thy pasture will give thee thanks
for ever: we will show forth thy
praise to all generations.*

PSALM 79:13

Living with Hope

When people receive a great gift, they usually cannot wait to tell everyone they know about it. Your mate is one of God's greatest blessings to you. Make sure other people know of your regard for your beloved. Don't keep your beloved's good qualities a secret. Speak of your blessings to others.

BLESSINGS

My beloved is . . . the chiefest among ten thousand.

SONG OF SOLOMON 5:10

Living with Hope

Love liberates. It can give you both wings to fly and a place to stand. Seek to give your mate courage and the space to grow into all that God has designed. Live a life of love and it will set you free.

LIBERATION

*And I will walk at liberty:
for I seek thy precepts.*

PSALM 119:45

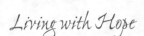

Living with Hope

Life can seem like a series of closed doors. Don't be afraid to ask to have the doors opened. God wants you and your beloved to seek what you want, and you will find it. That is His generous promise to you.

SEEKING

The heart of the prudent getteth knowledge; and the ear of the wise seeketh knowledge.

PROVERBS 18:15

Living with Hope

Focus your heart on the heart
of God, and He will work
miracles in your love life.
Seek to follow God's example
as you relate to your loved
one. He will bless you as
your minds and hearts
are stayed on Him.

FOCUS

*O God, my heart is fixed; I will sing
and give praise, even with my glory.*

PSALM 108:1

Living with Hope

Let your mind savor
sweetness, whether it is a
sweet thought of your beloved
or a sweet moment with the
Lord. Soak your being in love
and let affection be the
hallmark that describes
your life.

SWEETNESS

*The wise in heart shall be called
prudent: and the sweetness of the
lips increaseth learning.*

PROVERBS 16:21

Living with Hope

When you truly love and are
loved by someone, there is
little need for secrets.
After all, most of your faults
and shortcomings are already
known to the other. The good
news is that those in love
accept each other anyway.

REVEALING

*He revealeth the deep and secret
things: he knoweth what is in
the darkness, and the light
dwelleth with him.*

DANIEL 2:22

Living with Hope

God is the surgeon who sees
the wounds—large or small—
in our spirits and can make
them well. He sees what we
seek to hide, and He knows
the worth of our love for
others. Let God be the
surgeon in your lives. Let
Him do whatever is necessary
to make you whole.

WEIGHS

*All the ways of a man are clean
in his own eyes; but the LORD
weigheth the spirits.*

PROVERBS 16:2

Living with Hope

If inner troubles plague your marriage don't give up. The One who has borne all your transgressions is also the One who gives you hope for a new tomorrow. He walks with you and your mate. He will never leave you or leave you comfortless. That's His promise to you. Believe it. Live your life *knowing it is true.*

TRANSGRESSIONS

Surely he hath borne our griefs,
and carried our sorrows:
yet we did esteem him stricken,
smitten of God, and afflicted.

ISAIAH 53:4

Living with Hope

Think about our Lord's birth
in a manger. Sing praises to
God for the wondrous way in
which He showed His endless
love to all of mankind.
Be thankful for the gift of
a mate who loves and cares
about this priceless gift.

GLORY

*Glory to God in the highest, and on
earth peace, good will toward men.*

LUKE 2:14

Living with Hope

Reflect on the miracle of Jesus'
birth and ask Him to continue
the miracle of love He has
begun inside of you. Renew
your vows with your mate.
Let this day be one of joy,
fulfillment, and hope.

MIRACLE

*Thou shalt have joy and gladness;
and many shall rejoice at his birth.*

LUKE 1:14

Living with Hope

Despair is only for a span of time. God can bring your heart to a place of rejoicing and gladness. Thank Him for the care He gives to all of His children. Four of the most comforting words in the English language are: *This too shall pass.* Don't despair . . . joy comes in the morning.

DESPAIR

O satisfy us early with thy mercy;
that we may rejoice and be
glad all our days.

PSALM 90:14

Living with Hope

Love bursts forth from your
heart and waters the days of
your beloved. You scarcely feel
the love leaving you. Then you
see the result. Love brings
forth life in barren wastelands.

LIFE

*How fair and how pleasant
art thou, O love, for delights!*

SONG OF SOLOMON 7:6

Living with Hope

Make your love a safe
sanctuary for you and your
beloved. Keep your relationship
with your mate healthy and
strong so it can be a place of
comfort and retreat from
the troubles of life.

SANCTUARY

*He that dwelleth in the secret place
of the Most High shall abide under
the shadow of the Almighty.*

PSALM 91:1

Living with Hope

Do not conform to the image
of the world in your marriage.
Spend time in God's Word and
learn to love as God has loved.
Be patient with your spouse
and nurture your mate as God
would. See that your values
reflect those of the Father.

IMAGE

*And be not conformed to this world:
but be ye transformed by the renewing
of your mind, that ye may prove
what is that good, and acceptable,
and perfect will of God.*

ROMANS 12:2

Living with Hope

Hope is a defense against
many troubles in your life.
Exercise hope as you talk
with your mate. Pray in faith,
believing God will answer
your prayers. Ground your
hope in His love.

HOPE

*Remember the word unto thy
servant, upon which thou hast
caused me to hope.*

PSALM 119:49

Living with Hope

Consider how God has guided
you and blessed your family.
Pray with your beloved for
God to direct your path each
day of the year. May God
grant to you and your mate
His very best this day and
every day to come.

CONSIDER

I thought on my ways. . . .
At midnight I will rise to give
thanks unto thee because of thy
righteous judgments.

PSALM 119:59–62

Facing Hard Times

Love is a fortress against troubles from all sides. It will withstand fierce storms if your relationship is sturdy and strong. Be strong together.

FORTRESS

Better is a dinner of herbs where love is, than a stalled ox and hatred therewith.

PROVERBS 15:17

Facing Hard Times

Develop a sense of oneness with your partner. Use disagreements to build your relationship by talking about problems when they occur. Don't let resentment build a wall between you. If you do, it can become a wedge that can split you apart.

ONENESS

And if a house be divided against itself, that house cannot stand.

MARK 3:25

Facing Hard Times

If you feel overwhelmed by
the storms in your relationship
with your beloved, don't
despair. Ask God to come into
the midst of your problems
and bring you His calm and
all-abiding peace to strengthen
your togetherness.

CALM

*And he saith unto them, "Why are
ye fearful, O ye of little faith?" Then
he arose, and rebuked the winds and
the sea; and there was a great calm.*

MATTHEW 8:26

Facing Hard Times

Give to your beloved until
the cup runs over. Don't wait
to get from your loved one
before *you* show your love.
When your beloved is
disappointed by life and its
cares, give your lover even
more love and support.

RUNS OVER

*The lips of knowledge
are a precious jewel.*

PROVERBS 20:15

Facing Hard Times

Make sure your actions match your words. Don't tell someone "I love you, oh, how I love you," and then neglect to show love in action and deed. Be kind and considerate with your loved one.

CONSIDERATION

Though I speak with the tongues of men and of angels, and have not charity, I am become as sounding brass, or a tinkling cymbal.

1 CORINTHIANS 13:1

Facing Hard Times

Commit yourself to the
promises of God in the hard
times. Don't give way to a
bottomless pit of despair.
Talk to God about your
feelings. Remind Him of the
promises He has made
to His people—to YOU!

COMMIT

*Blessed is the man that endureth
temptation: for when he is tried,
he shall receive the crown of life,
which the Lord hath promised
to them that love him.*

JAMES 1:12

Facing Hard Times

Don't underestimate the
power of love to see you
through the hard times.
Faith and hope are vital. But
the Bible tells us that love
continues to win the day.
Tell your mate of your love
even more when the hard
times come.

CHARITY

*And now abideth faith, hope,
charity, these three; but the
greatest of these is charity.*

1 CORINTHIANS 13:13

253

Facing Hard Times

Be grateful for these times
with your mate that are filled
with richness, quietness and
contentment. Don't let the
pursuit of money or fame
become a substitute for
spending time nourishing
your love relationship.

QUIETNESS

*In returning and rest shall ye
be saved; in quietness and in
confidence shall be your strength.*

ISAIAH 30:15

Facing Hard Times

Look for times in your
love relationship when you
can speak a word of
encouragement or praise.
Don't hesitate to tell of the
joy you share with your loved
one. Positive words strengthen
the bond of love you share.

POSITIVE

*A man hath joy by the answer
of his mouth: and a word spoken
in due season, how good is it!*

PROVERBS 15:23

Facing Hard Times

Don't be misled. Adultery can never be hidden. The effects show in your life, and your mate will know of your betrayal, even if it's only in the guilt you are trying to hide.

FIRE

Can a man take fire in his bosom, and his clothes not be burned? . . . So he that goeth in to his neighbor's wife; whosoever toucheth her shall not be innocent.

PROVERBS 6:27–29

Facing Hard Times

Remember, you don't have to face your troubles alone. God is on the side of His children, and He will stand with you as you face the obstacles in your life. Nor are you alone in your physical relationship. Stand strong with your beloved.

ENEMIES

Through God we shall do valiantly: for he it is that shall tread down our enemies.

PSALM 108:13

257

Facing Hard Times

Seek to find peace in the troubles and challenges of your relationship. Remember, love is not a contest, it is an exciting, cooperative venture that explores the uncharted worlds of relationship. Blessed is the one who makes peace.

STRIFE

*It is an honor for a man
to cease from strife.*

PROVERBS 20:3

Facing Hard Times

Be careful about having
too many secrets from your
mate. Learn to be open and
vulnerable. Openness develops
trust, and trust builds love.
Ask God for courage to be
transparently YOU with
the one you love.

SECRETS

*By humility and the fear of the Lord
are riches, and honor, and life.*

PROVERBS 22:4

Facing Hard Times

Come to God boldly. Ask Him
what you need to have in your
relationship with your beloved.
The path of love will at times
be rough indeed. Ask God to
help you smooth the way.
All you have to do is ask.

BOLDLY

*Let us therefore come boldly unto
the throne of grace, that we may
obtain mercy, and find grace
to help in time of need.*

HEBREWS 4:16

Facing Hard Times

Being angry is not a sin.
However, be careful that
your anger does not lead you
to sin. Talk about your fears,
frustrations, and hurts with
your beloved. Don't hold
your anger inside.

FRUSTRATION

*Be ye angry, and sin not; let not the
sun go down upon your wrath.*

EPHESIANS 4:26

Facing Hard Times

True love outlasts the most
difficult of times. Nourish your
love in the hard times. It will
make your troubles more
bearable. Learn to stand close
to your beloved when storms
shake your household.

TENDERNESS

*Peace I leave with you, my peace
I give unto you. . . . Let not your heart
be troubled, neither let it be afraid.*

JOHN 14:27

Facing Hard Times

God replaces your losses
with good things. If you are
following Him and lose
someone close to you, always
remember how much He
cares, and that He has
promised to fill your aching
void with His special love.

LOSSES

*I will be glad and rejoice in thy
mercy: for thou hast considered
my trouble; thou hast known
my soul in adversities.*

PSALM 31:7

Facing Hard Times

Love doesn't just happen.
It's God who gives us the
power to love. If you find it
difficult to express love, ask
God for His direction and
insight. He will give you the
ability and the wisdom to love
better and stronger than you
ever dreamed possible.

WISE ONE

*He that loveth not, knoweth
not God; for God is love.*

1 JOHN 4:8

Facing Hard Times

Don't be misled. If you commit adultery, you are doing more than just harming the relationship you share with your mate. You are doing what may be irreparable damage to your very soul. The guilt and deceit can eat away at your conscience until you are consumed.

DESTRUCTION

But whoso committeth adultery with a woman lacketh understanding: he that doeth it destroyeth his own soul.

PROVERBS 6:32

Facing Hard Times

Learn to be joyful and relish
the love that you have
with your mate. Don't let
troubles rob you of an
exuberant happiness in being
together. Hug your lover and
talk of your special feelings.
Do it right now! Do it often!

RELISH

*Live joyfully with the wife
whom thou lovest. . . .*

ECCLESIASTES 9:9

Facing Hard Times

When it seems like your
troubles beat against you
relentlessly, remember God
has promised to be your
shade. He has promised to
refresh you in the battles
you face and to keep you.

SHADE

*The Lord is thy keeper: the Lord
is thy shade upon thy right hand.*

PSALM 121:5

Facing Hard Times

If you have problems, don't wait to take them to God. You cannot face your hard times alone. Ask God to intervene and give you wisdom. He will stand with you in each situation. Together—you and your mate—take your problems and concerns to the Lord in earnest prayer.

ALONE

They cried unto the LORD in their trouble, and he delivered them out of their distresses.

PSALM 107:6

Facing Hard Times

If you and your mate are
afraid and nervous, remember
God has promised to send
His angels and His Holy Spirit
to watch over you. Do not
worry, God is in charge and
He loves you both more
than you'll ever know.

NERVOUS

*For he shall give his angels charge
over thee, to keep thee in all thy ways.*

PSALM 91:11

Facing Hard Times

God specializes in new
beginnings for couples.
In the historic past as much
as in the present, God has
given new dreams to couples
and has stood with them as
those cherished dreams
came true. Don't be afraid
to ask God for a new
plan for your future.

DREAMS

And God said unto Abraham,
As for Sarai . . . I will bless her,
and give thee a son also of her: yea,
I will bless her, and she shall be
a mother of nations; kings of people
shall be of her.

GENESIS 17:15–16

Facing Hard Times

Don't be a martyr to your mate. Give from a joyful heart and not as one who is forced to make sacrifices. Remember, true, abiding love comes from the heart, not from the bank account.

SACRIFICES

Better it is to be of a humble spirit with the lowly, than to divide the spoil with the proud.

PROVERBS 16:19

Facing Hard Times

If it's been a while since you and your mate have turned to God and really listened to Him, don't despair. It's never too late for the repentant heart to seek His face. Do it together. Call on Him today.

RETURNING

Turn us again, O God, and cause thy face to shine; and we shall be saved.

PSALM 80:3

Facing Hard Times

When you and your mate
come before God, don't
pretend you are satisfied
when you are not. Talk over
any misunderstandings you
may have with one another.
God longs for honesty from
His people who want to get
to know Him more completely.

HONESTY

*For he satisfieth the longing soul, and
filleth the hungry soul with goodness.*

PSALM 107:9

Facing Hard Times

When you are facing hard times, don't worry if you seem to be weak and helpless. God promises to give you His strength to do what you need to do. Pray to your loving Father and ask Him to bring strength to your weakness.

STRENGTH

I will go in the strength of the Lord GOD: I will make mention of thy righteousness, even of thine only.

PSALM 71:16

Facing Hard Times

When you grieve, it's all right
to weep. But don't weep as
those couples who have no
hope. The God of all creation
listens to you when you
mourn, and He has promised
to comfort you and bless
you with good things.

GRIEF

*He that goeth forth and weepeth,
bearing precious seed, shall doubtless
come again with rejoicing, bringing
his sheaves with him.*

PSALM 126:6

Growing with God

Go to bed tonight with blissful thoughts of what God has done and is doing in your marriage and in your family life. Give thanks to Him and to your spouse for the happiness you are enjoying each day. Praise Him for your love together.

BLISSFUL

The LORD hath done great things for us; whereof we are glad.

PSALM 126:3

Growing with God

If you are impatient with God's work in your love relationship, don't hesitate to tell Him the concerns of your heart. Right now, tell God you want a relationship that is meaningful and fulfilling for both you and your spouse. Ask Him to make your love stronger each day.

CHANGES

Let thine hand help me;
for I have chosen thy precepts.

PSALM 119:173

Growing with God

Honesty is one of the most
vital ingredients to a loving
relationship. If you are afraid
of being fully known by your
beloved, practice by first being
vulnerable before God. Share
deeply with Him. Tell Him
things unknown to others.
Once you feel His boundless
acceptance, you'll find yourself
better prepared to be honest
with your beloved.

VULNERABLE

Search me, O God,
and know my heart: try me,
and know my thoughts.

PSALM 139:23

Growing with God

When you feel hurt or
unloved, you may want to hit
back. In your heart, you know
that revenge doesn't build
love. Talk about your hurts
and disappointments with
your beloved. Love your
spouse today as never before.

REVENGE

*Dearly beloved, avenge not yourselves,
but rather give place unto wrath:
for it is written, Vengeance is mine:
I will repay, saith the Lord.*

ROMANS 12:19

279

Growing with God

Does your beloved seem far away, lost in concerns and problems? Everyone feels alone at times—uncared for and seemingly without a friend. Remember, that's one of the best times to draw nigh to God. He is your friend and constant companion.

CUDDLE

*Draw nigh to God,
and he will draw nigh to you.*

JAMES 4:8

Growing with God

Set aside a regular time to read God's Word with your beloved. As your souls grow closer to God, you will find yourselves growing closer to each other. Make *shared devotions once a day* a vital part of your relationship and your spiritual growth together.

DEVOTIONS

Search the Scriptures; for in them ye think ye have eternal life: and they are they which testify of me.

JOHN 5:39

Growing with God

Rejoice in the pleasures
God has given you in your
marriage. Thank Him for the
abundance of affection and
passion with which He has
blessed you. Remember how
He smiles when you drink
deeply of His gifts.

PLEASURES

*They shall be abundantly satisfied
with the fatness of thy house;
and thou shalt make them drink
of the river of thy pleasures.*

PSALM 36:8

Growing with God

If you wish you had greater comprehension of your beloved, yourself, and others, don't despair. God has promised His boundless wisdom to those who come to Him in faith—believing. Ask God to open your eyes. In so doing, you'll be like the blind man in the Bible who simply said, "Once I was blind, but now I can see." Ask God for that sight—and insight—today.

COMPREHENSION

Open thou mine eyes, that
I may behold wondrous things
out of thy law.

PSALM 119:18

Growing with God

Keep your eyes focused on the
positive, good things in your
love relationship—the qualities
that brought you together in
the first place. Look for ways
to compliment your beloved.
A single word of praise
does more good than pages
of well-meant criticism.

LOVINGKINDNESS

*For thy lovingkindness is before mine
eyes; and I have walked in thy truth.*

PSALM 26:3

Growing with God

The loyalty you feel for your
beloved is precious beyond
words. Tell your mate you will
"stand fast" all the way.
It is easy to be gracious,
when you're riding the crest
of personal success. Be there
for the hard times, too.

LOYALTY

*And Ruth said, Entreat me not to
leave thee, or to return from following
after thee: for whither thou goest,
I will go; and where thou lodgest,
I will lodge: thy people shall be my
people, and thy God my God.*

RUTH 1:16

Growing with God

Laugh joyously with your
beloved. Lift your eyes to the
sky and praise God for the
light He has given to you in
your love life together.
He directs you in plentiful
paths. Walk them with
joy and gladness.

LAUGHTER

*Light is sown for the righteous,
and gladness for the upright in heart.*

PSALM 97:11

Growing with God

Speak your emotions freely.
Your love will flourish as a
result of the outpouring of
your heart. The same is true in
your relationship with God.
He wants you to tell Him how
you feel. Speak your mind.
Share your heart. God will
listen and comfort you in
all your ways.

OPENNESS

*I cried with my whole heart; hear me,
O LORD: I will keep thy statutes.*

PSALM 119:145

Growing with God

Seek to love your mate with all
the fruits of the Spirit. Let your
relationship be a model for all
others to see—especially if
you have a child. If you lack
any of the fruits, ask of the
One who gives abundantly
to all who seek. Our God is
loving and generous.
Ask and you will receive.

FRUITS

*But the fruit of the Spirit is love,
joy, peace, longsuffering, gentleness,
goodness, faith, meekness, temperance:
against such there is no law.*

GALATIANS 5:22, 23

Growing with God

You can't earn love. Love is
a gift. You can't buy love. It's
simply not for sale. And it's
especially true for God's love.
God has given us love because
He has chosen to do so.
No one has ever been good
enough or rich enough to earn
His love. So it is with your
spouse. No one is ever good
enough to receive love.
We love simply because we
choose to love. Unconditional
love is the most powerful
force on earth.

CHOICE

He delivered me,
because he delighted in me.

PSALM 18:19

Growing with God

If you have a love thought for
your beloved, speak it now!
There are no guarantees from
day to day. Take the time today
to express your love. Live
today with your love as
though this were the last.

REGRET

*For all flesh is as grass, and all the
glory of man as the flower of grass.
The grass withereth, and the flower
thereof falleth away: but the word
of the Lord endureth forever. . . .*

1 PETER 1:24–25

Growing with God

The Bible says we are all equally precious in the eyes of God. Put your beloved's concerns on an equal footing with your own. Search for the best in your spouse. In so doing, your love relationship will flourish. Enjoy the dream of staying in love—forever.

EQUALS

There is neither Jew nor Greek, there is neither bond nor free, there is neither male nor female: for ye are all one in Christ Jesus.

GALATIANS 3:28

Growing with God

Share your deepest reflections
with your beloved. Talk often
of the things on your mind
and your heart. The more you
share, the closer you'll come
to each other in love and
understanding. Give the one
you love the gift of yourself.

REFLECTIONS

*How precious also are thy
thoughts unto me, O God!
How great is the sum of them!*

Growing with God

Conceit is a dangerous
ingredient in a love
relationship. You are walking
on eggshells when you begin
to feel you are the only one
who knows or understands
the situation. Chances are
you'll soon find yourself
alone with your store of
knowledge. Always look
at both sides of the issue.
It still takes two to tango.

CONCEIT

*Seest thou a man wise in his
own conceit? There is more hope
of a fool than of him.*

PROVERBS 26:12

Growing with God

Love your spouse and ask God to make your love blossom into a tree that shades your life with goodness and contentment. Do not count the cost of love, look only to the end result of your togetherness.

BLOSSOM

Many waters cannot quench love, neither can the floods drown it.

SONG OF SOLOMON 8:7

Growing with God

Pray for your love relationship
with the confidence that God
will give you the desires
of your heart. God listens
to the pleas and your deepest
concerns. His ears are waiting
to hear your inner desires.
He cares about you
and your beloved.

WAITING

*For the eyes of the Lord are over
the righteous, and his ears are
open unto their prayers.*

1 PETER 3:12

Growing with God

The Bible says the harmony
of your love life affects the
working of your prayers.
God does not respond to your
supplications the same if you
pray from one side of your
mouth while fighting with
your mate out of the other.
Let your life together be
one of harmony.

TOGETHERNESS

*Likewise, ye husbands, dwell with
them according to knowledge, giving
honor unto the wife, as unto the
weaker vessel, and as being heirs
together of the grace of life; that your
prayers be not hindered.*

1 PETER 3:7

Growing with God

Build up your beloved in the
faith of our Lord Jesus Christ.
Encourage your mate with
prayer and the witness of
what God has done in your
own life. Together grow in the
knowledge of Him, His love,
and His goodness.

BUILD

*But ye, beloved, building up
yourselves on your most holy faith,
praying in the Holy Ghost, keep
yourselves in the love of God,
looking for the mercy of our
Lord Jesus Christ unto eternal life.*

JUDE 20, 21

Growing with God

Study the Scriptures. Meditate
on God's Word. Read His
promises together with your
beloved and talk about what
His divine counsel means in
your everyday life. The Bible
is as fresh today as when it
was first given to humankind.
Let it be your guide in your
own loving relationship
with your spouse.

PURE

*The words of the LORD are pure
words: as silver tried in a furnace
of earth, purified seven times.*

PSALM 12:6

Growing with God

The farmer does not have
a harvest the day after
planting. A good crop takes
time, patience, and tender,
loving care. It's akin to your
relationship with your spouse.
God is working to draw you
and your beloved closer
together *and to Him!*

GROWTH

Verily, verily, I say unto you,
Except a corn of wheat fall into the
ground and die, it abideth alone:
but if it die, it bringeth
forth much fruit.

JOHN 12:24

Growing with God

By your example of love and caring, love your unbelieving mate into a relationship with God. Intrigue your spouse with words consistent with your loving actions. Show your beloved what a difference God continues to make in your own life. Love your mate into embracing the gospel.

WITNESSING

For what knowest thou, O wife, whether thou shalt save thy husband? or how knowest thou, O man, whether thou shalt save thy wife?

1 CORINTHIANS 7:16

Growing with God

Celebrate every success with
your mate. Lift your arms
and give thanks. Embrace the
peaks of joy and happiness.
God is in all good things.
Applaud your mate's
achievements with
enthusiasm. Join together
in thanksgiving.

SUCCESS

*Let another man praise thee,
and not thine own mouth.*

PROVERBS 27:2

Growing with God

The beginnings of love are like a vapor. There may be times when it will seem easier to just let it blow away. But God puts His angels before you and desires to stop the vapor from disappearing. Ask Him to keep your love alive. He wants the best for the two of you as you continue to share your life living and loving together.

BEGINNINGS

To be carnally minded is death;
but to be spiritually minded
is life and peace.

ROMANS 8:6

Growing with God

Treat your love like a precious
jewel. Gaze at the sparkling
stone but do not smash it to
see how it's been created.
Leave some room for mystery.
Let your love be a constant
unraveling of the good things
between you.

JEWEL

*Let me see thy countenance, let me
hear thy voice; for sweet is thy voice,
and thy countenance is comely.*

SONG OF SOLOMON 2:14

Growing with God

God binds up the rejected.
If your beloved turns from
you, know that you will be
comforted in the arms of our
heavenly Father. He grieves
with those who grieve, and
He comforts all who turn to
Him. Rejection is painful.
But whatever does not
kill you *makes you stronger.*

COMFORT

*For the LORD hath called thee
as a woman forsaken and grieved
in spirit, and a wife of youth, when
thou wast refused, saith thy God.*

ISAIAH 54:6

Growing with God

God will always welcome you
with open arms. No request is
too small or too big to bring to
Him. Tell our gracious Lord all
that is on your heart regarding
the one you love. Learn to
pray for that which is difficult.
While praying, anticipate God
doing the impossible.

ANTICIPATION

*Thou art my hiding place; thou
shalt preserve me from trouble;
thou shalt compass me about
with songs of deliverance.*

PSALM 32:7

Rejoicing in Abundance

The Lord of all the heavens
and earth has blessed you
with His love and care.
He delights in pleasing you
throughout your days and
in helping you and your
beloved grow to full stature.

GROWING

*I will sing unto the LORD, because
he hath dealt bountifully with me.*

PSALM 13:6

Rejoicing in Abundance

Give and it shall be given back
to you, pressed down and
overflowing. An open heart
and a gentle, open hand are
the best insurances of a long
and lasting love affair with
your mate.

OVERFLOWING

*The liberal soul shall be made fat:
and he that watereth shall be watered
also himself.*

PROVERBS 11:25

Rejoicing in Abundance

God rains down His anointing
power on His people. If you or
your spouse have any lack,
go to the Father who knows
your every need. He will
open His great storehouse
of blessings and shower you
with His generous heart.

ANOINTING

*Thou anointest my head with oil;
my cup runneth over. Surely goodness
and mercy shall follow me all the
days of my life; and I will dwell
in the house of the LORD forever.*

PSALM 23:5–6

Rejoicing in Abundance

A smile can warm the coldest
heart. Think on good things,
and your smile will radiate
a contentment that will draw
others to you. Adding more
smiles to your marriage
inevitably adds more
romance to your life.

SMILES

*A merry heart doeth good like
a medicine: but a broken spirit
drieth the bones.*

PROVERBS 17:22

Rejoicing in Abundance

If you and your spouse were to count all the wondrous things God has done for you, you would soon be overwhelmed. He gave you life, sustenance, and continues to share with you His all-abiding love. He also gave you a mind and a heart to appreciate all He has given.

GIFTS

Come and hear, all ye that fear God, and I will declare what he hath done for my soul.

PSALM 66:16

Rejoicing in Abundance

Get a grip on hope, and hang
on tight. Hope is the rope that
rescues us from despair and
lethargy. Hang on tight, and
keep expecting God to work
a miracle in your life.

HANG ON

*But I will hope continually, and will
yet praise thee more and more.*

PSALM 71:14

Rejoicing in Abundance

Compliments bring a sparkle
to everyone's eyes. Be a
person who looks for reasons
to compliment your beloved.
Notice the fabric of your
spouse's personality and
give all the encouragement
and praise you can.

PRAISE

*The light of the eyes rejoiceth
the heart: and a good report
maketh the bones fat.*

PROVERBS 15:30

Rejoicing in Abundance

God's hand flung the moon
into space and set the sun
in its orbit. He holds the stars
in His power and moves the
seas at His whim. Rejoice in
the special love He has created
for you and your beloved.

CREATION

*The day is thine, the night also
is thine: thou hast prepared the
light and the sun.*

PSALM 74:16

Rejoicing in Abundance

Love your mate with
abandonment. Don't measure
your love and weigh what you
receive in return. Be a lover
who gives yourself today with
no thought for the hurts
of the past or the problems
of the future.

UNMEASURED

Give, and it shall be given unto you;
good measure, pressed down, and
shaken together, and running over,
shall men give into your bosom.

LUKE 6:38

Rejoicing in Abundance

If you feel alone and
insignificant, don't despair.
God lifts up the humble
and comforts those who are
abandoned. Bring your heart
to Him for healing and
new hope.

ENDURANCE

*I watch, and am as a sparrow alone
upon the housetop. . . . But thou,
O LORD, shalt endure for ever; and thy
remembrance unto all generations.*

PSALM 102:7, 12

Rejoicing in Abundance

God has put His loving hand
on the pulse of your life, and
He has given you wondrous
gifts. Thank Him for the gift
of love He has given to you
through your special mate.

FAVOR

*Whoso findeth a wife findeth
a good thing, and obtaineth
favor of the LORD.*

PROVERBS 18:22

Rejoicing in Abundance

Savor each day and drink
of its sweetness. Treasure each
moment of vibrant life the
Lord has given to you. Don't
wile away your hours or your
days waiting for what will be.
Enjoy what is. Do it now!

ENJOY!

*This is the day which the LORD
hath made; we will rejoice
and be glad in it.*

PSALM 118:24

Rejoicing in Abundance

God has spread His mantle
of protection over your family.
He loves the ones you love
even more than you do.
Come to Him as a family, and
ask for the grace you each
need to live out your days.

GRACE

*The LORD shall increase you more
and more, you and your children.*

PSALM 115:14

Rejoicing in Abundance

Lift your arms to the sky and
thank God for the sunshine
He has given to you. Every
ounce of energy you have
has been given to you by Him.
Rejoice in the abundance of
health and wealth He has
given you and your beloved.

PROSPER

*Beloved, I wish above all things
that thou mayest prosper and be in
health, even as thy soul prospereth.*

3 JOHN 1:2

Rejoicing in Abundance

Your words of love are a
sweet nectar to your beloved.
Pour love words on the heart
of your mate until you are
both satiated. Celebrate your
love and be enormously
happy together.

SATIATED

*Behold, thou art fair, my love;
behold, thou art fair.*

SONG OF SOLOMON 1:15

Rejoicing in Abundance

God has woven threads
of gold throughout your life.
Don't hesitate to remind
yourself and others of the
good things God has done for
you in the past. It gives you
reason to hope. Explore the
good of days gone by . . .
enjoy your past heritage
and share it with others.

TESTIMONIES

*Thy testimonies have I taken
as a heritage for ever: for they are
the rejoicing of my heart.*

PSALM 119:111

Rejoicing in Abundance

Crown your life with honor.
Be careful that scandal doesn't
rightfully attach to your name.
Live your life honestly, and you
and your beloved will enjoy
peace in all your dealings.

HONOR

*But above all things, my brethren,
swear not, neither by heaven, neither
by the earth, neither by any other
oath; but let your yea be yea;
and your nay, nay; lest ye fall
into condemnation.*

JAMES 5:12

Rejoicing in Abundance

Pour warm laughter over your life with your beloved. Ask the Father, who delights in each of us, to teach you to delight in the ways of each other as children delight in each new day's discoveries.

DELIGHT

He brought me forth also into a large place: he delivered me, because he delighted in me.

2 SAMUEL 22:20

Rejoicing in Abundance

Love is a great treasure hunt.
Seek to discover the priceless
and the special facets of your
beloved's heart and soul. One
way to discover the treasures
of your spouse is to read
God's Word together and
meditate on His love.

PRICELESS

*I rejoice at thy word, as one
that findeth great spoil.*

PSALM 119:162

324

Rejoicing in Abundance

Love your mate with an active, emotional love. Hear the joys and the sadness of the one you love. Remind your beloved of your steadfast love during the challenging times of your life.

EMOTIONAL

Then said Elkanah her husband to her, Hannah, why weepest thou? and why eatest thou not? and why is thy heart grieved? am not I better to thee than ten sons?

1 SAMUEL 1:8

Rejoicing in Abundance

Refresh yourself with the love
you share with your heart's
partner. Shape your love into
the same kind of love God
gives to each of you. May your
affection be a shade tree
during life's dry seasons.

REFRESH

*The LORD is thy shade upon thy
right hand. The sun shall not smite
thee by day, nor the moon by night.*

PSALM 121:5–6

Rejoicing in Abundance

Feel the texture of your
beloved's spirit. Spend time
together in prayer so you
know the soul of your mate
as well as you know your
own. It takes time . . . but you
will be richer as a result
of your caring.

SOUL

*And fear not them which kill the
body, but are not able to kill the soul:
but rather fear him which is able to
destroy both soul and body in hell.*

MATTHEW 10:28

Rejoicing in Abundance

Develop a thankful heart.
Look for reasons to be
thankful to God and to your
mate. A thankful tongue will
water your relationship until
love will blossom beyond
your greatest expectations.

THANKFUL

*Let the heavens rejoice, and let
the earth be glad; let the sea roar,
and the fulness thereof.*

PSALM 96:11

Rejoicing in Abundance

Offer criticism cautiously.
In any relationship, there are
two sides to every issue.
Examine your own actions
before you turn a critical eye
to the actions of your mate.
Your task is to love, not
criticize. If you need to
change your perspective, start
changing today, not tomorrow.

PERSPECTIVE

*And why beholdest thou the
mote that is in thy brother's eye,
but perceivest not the beam that
is in thine own eye?*

LUKE 6:41

Rejoicing in Abundance

Forgiveness can make the sun
shine on a marriage in trouble.
It will make love sprout and
grow in ground that once
seemed barren. Don't bear
grudges against your beloved.
Freely forgive.

FORGIVENESS

*For thou, Lord, art good, and ready to
forgive; and plenteous in mercy unto
all them that call upon thee.*

PSALM 86:5

Rejoicing in Abundance

The ongoing challenges of life
can place heavy burdens on
you and your mate. Learn to
lift the weight together so the
troubles do not crush either of
you. Almost any burden, when
shared equally, can be borne.
Flex your muscles together.
The load will be lighter.

TROUBLES

They helped every one his neighbor;
and every one said to his brother,
Be of good courage.

ISAIAH 41:6

Rejoicing in Abundance

Give praise unto God. Hold hands with your beloved and stand before the Almighty in gratitude for who He is and what He has done in your own private world. Keep your eyes focused on Him, and He will give you a peace beyond understanding.

GRATITUDE

I will praise thee, O LORD, with my whole heart; I will show forth all thy marvelous works.

PSALM 9:1

Rejoicing in Abundance

Loneliness is a dark place.
Emptiness seems to surround
you. Then your beloved enters.
The love of your spouse is a
bright and glowing candle that
lights every corner of your
solitary aloneness.

BRIGHTNESS

*I am my beloved's,
and his desire is toward me.*

SONG OF SOLOMON 7:10

Rejoicing in Abundance

Little words, like "Please forgive" or "I care" will make a big difference in your marriage. Don't neglect the seemingly little words; they speak richly of your special love and attention.

LITTLE THINGS

A word fitly spoken is like apples of gold in pictures of silver.

PROVERBS 25:11

Building a Family

If you yearn for children and
have none of your own, come
to God in prayer. God delights
in giving you good things.
Ask Him to bless you with
a child to love and to cherish.

CHILDREN

*He maketh the barren woman to
keep house, and to be a joyful mother
of children. Praise ye the LORD.*

Building a Family

If you want your child to
grow to be a God-fearing man
or woman, then you and your
mate need to show him what
God-fearing people live like.
There is no substitute for
a loving example. Be that
example of God's love today.

EXAMPLE

*Blessed is the man that feareth
the LORD, that delighteth greatly
in his commandments.*

PSALM 112:1

Building a Family

It is important to teach your
child the law and the love
of God. Read the Scriptures
together as a family. Give
your child the chance to ask
questions about your own
beliefs. Say in words he
can understand what God
has done in the life of you
and your mate.

LAW

*My son, hear the instruction
of thy father, and forsake not the law
of thy mother: for they shall be an
ornament of grace unto thy head,
and chains about thy neck.*

PROVERBS 1:8–9

Building a Family

Discipline is a difficult area
for many families. Discuss
with your mate how you both
wish to deal with the various
areas of challenge in raising
children. Then be both firm
and compassionate in your
daily discipline—always speak
the truth in love.

DISCIPLINE

*For whom the LORD loveth he
correcteth; even as a father the
son in whom he delighteth.*

PROVERBS 3:12

Building a Family

Have hope as you nurture
your child. The Bible says the
early training will abide with
him even when he is old.
Make it a happy habit to talk
with your child at an early
age about God's love.

TRAINING

Train up a child in the way he
should go: and when he is old,
he will not depart from it.

PROVERBS 22:6

Building a Family

Faith is contagious. When you and your spouse speak of your faith and live it in your everyday lives, your child will be influenced by its power. Show your child how to have faith today.

FAITH

When I call to remembrance the unfeigned faith that is in thee, which dwelt first in thy grandmother Lois, and thy mother Eunice; and I am persuaded that in thee also.

2 TIMOTHY 1:5

Building a Family

Teach your child to tell the truth. A respect for honesty will serve him well throughout his entire life. Be sure to speak the truth yourself in your dealings with others.
Your child will see it and follow your example.

TRUTH

I have no greater joy than to hear that my children walk in truth.

3 JOHN 1:4

Building a Family

Guide your child with gentleness and kindness. Show your child kindness from an early age, and train him with a godly affection. Even when you must discipline, be sure your child knows he is loved simply for who he is.

GENTLENESS

But we were gentle among you, even as a nurse cherisheth her children.

1 THESSALONIANS 2:7

Building a Family

Teach your child to obey you.
Early lessons in respect for
authority provide your child
with a firm base for success
in relationships with others.
When you are affectionate
with your child, it is easier
for him to want to do
what you say.

OBEDIENCE

*Children, obey your parents
in the Lord: for this is right.*

EPHESIANS 6:1

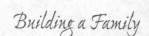

Building a Family

Don't be so stern with your
child that you cause him to
be angry and rebellious. Make
every human effort to be fair
and just in your rules and
expectations, and always
handle your discipline
with love.

REBELLION

*Fathers, provoke not your children
to anger, lest they be discouraged.*

COLOSSIANS 3:21

Building a Family

When you train your child well, you will bear pleasant fruit in later years. A wise and righteous child will bring joy to the hearts of yourself and your spouse. Encourage your child in the ways of wisdom.

WISDOM

The father of the righteous shall greatly rejoice: and he that begetteth a wise child shall have joy of him.

PROVERBS 23:24

Building a Family

The soul of your child is a
precious trust from the Lord.
God wants each of His children
to come to know Him. Teach
your child of God's love, and
pray for his eternal salvation.

ETERNAL SOUL

*Even so it is not the will of your
Father which is in heaven, that one
of these little ones should perish.*

MATTHEW 18:14

Building a Family

Leave a legacy for your child. When you have children, you immediately begin to care more deeply about the care and feeding of the nation and our physical world. Talk with your spouse about what you two can do to help make our planet a better place for your child to live.

LEGACY

One generation shall praise thy works to another, and shall declare thy mighty acts.

PSALM 145:4

Building a Family

Don't underestimate your child. The natural dependency and openness of a child is so precious that Jesus said it was childlike people who made up His kingdom. Encourage your child to keep the enthusiasm of his early days—so that it may serve him well as he grows into an adult.

ENTHUSIASM

But Jesus said, "Suffer little children, and forbid them not, to come unto me; for of such is the kingdom of heaven."

MATTHEW 19:14

Building a Family

God has made a commitment
to you, your spouse, and
your child. If you follow Him,
He will remember you and
redeem you. Be a gentle guide
to your whole family as
you yourself follow His
counsel today.

COVENANT

*He hath remembered his covenant for
ever, the word which he commanded
to a thousand generations.*

PSALM 105:8

Building a Family

Your child is a heritage from
the Lord. He has placed your
child in your care to delight
you and to challenge you
to grow into the person
He wants you to be.

HERITAGE

*Lo, children are a heritage of the
LORD: and the fruit of the womb
is his reward.*

PSALM 127:3

Building a Family

Your child is a blessing from God. He's given him to you for your love and nurture. Show him the way of God's truth. Let your life and love point your child to the Lord.

INSTRUCTION

My son, hear the instruction of thy father, . . .

Building a Family

God is the champion of children. It is an honor to have Him give a child into your care and the care of your spouse. But He also stands with you as you struggle to raise your children.

STRUGGLES

Whosoever shall offend one of these little ones that believe in me, it is better for him that a millstone were hanged about his neck, and he were cast into the sea.

MARK 9:42